HORRIBLE

TWO
HORRIBLE
BOOKS IN
ONE

THE ANGRY
AZTECS
AND
THE INCREDIBLE
INCAS

Terry Deary ✷ Martin Brown
Philip Reeve

■SCHOLASTIC

Scholastic Children's Books,
Euston House, 24 Eversholt Street,
London NW1 1DB, UK

A division of Scholastic Ltd
London ~ New York ~ Toronto ~ Sydney ~ Auckland
Mexico City ~ New Delhi ~ Hong Kong

Published in this edition by Scholastic Ltd, 2004
Cover illustration copyright © Martin Brown, 2001

The Angry Aztecs
First published in the UK by Scholastic Ltd, 1997
Text copyright © Terry Deary, 1997
Illustrations copyright © Martin Brown, 1997

The Incredible Incas
First published in the UK by Scholastic Ltd, 2000
Text copyright © Terry Deary, 2000
Illustrations copyright © Philip Reeve, 2000

10 digit ISBN 0 439 96802 X
13 digit ISBN 978 0439 96802 7

Printed in the UK by CPI Bookmarque, Croydon, CR0 4TD

6 8 10 9 7

Contents

THE ANGRY
AZTECS

For Aidan Doyle

INTRODUCTION

History can be horrible. Horribly foul facts and fouler figures, dusty dates and dustier dead people, lousy laws and lousier wars.

Now's the time for a revolution – not the French Revolution, the American Revolution, or even the rotten Russian Revolution but ... the Classroom Revolution!

Of course, a revolution needs weapons. So here is a classified secret. A secret so terrible that it is only whispered in staffrooms around the world. It is the answer to every pupil's question ...

What is the weapon that every teacher fears more than anything in the world?

No! It's not the smell of Billy Brown's socks!

No! It's not the taste of school-dinner skunk-burgers!

No! It's not the head teacher finding the brandy in the book cupboard!

It is . . . a question!

It is . . . the question 'Why?'

Try it for yourself . . . but only use the 'Why Weapon' against a nasty teacher who deserves it. And keep on using it till they break down and admit they do not know the answer!

Here is an example . . .

See? Not only do you get revenge on your horrible history teacher . . . you also start to explore the really, really interesting thing about history. The question, 'Why did people behave the way they did?'

If you can answer that then you can begin to understand the question, 'Why do people behave the way they do now?' And, in the end you answer the only question that matters in life: 'Why do I behave the way I do?'

Hopefully this Horrible History book will help you to understand a little bit about history . . . but an awful lot about PEOPLE!

TERRIBLE TIMELINE

The good news is that the world won't end tomorrow.

The bad news is that it is going to end on 22 December 2012. (So I hope you're a fast reader, otherwise you'll be seriously dead before you finish reading this book and you'll have wasted your money.)

In case you are interested in how you are going to die I can tell you that there will be disastrous earthquakes. If the cracks in the earth don't swallow you up then the terrible shaking that your brain cells get will give you a fatal headache. (It might be a good idea to stock up on aspirin now!)

How do we know this cheerful bit of information? Because an ancient people called the Maya worked it out. They could read the stars like you can read the *Sun* (newspaper that is). And the stars say that's when the world will end.

These Mayan people were just one bunch of some remarkable old South American nations who were a bit like hedgehogs on a motorway – they didn't have wheels (they never got around to it) and were flattened by people who did.

The other interesting Central American Indians are called Aztecs and they lived in an area we call Mexico today. They moved in as next-door neighbours to the Maya (in Yucatan) and naturally learned quite a lot from them.

The Aztecs were the neighbours from Hell. Within a few hundred years they had made themselves the top tribe in Mexico. Nobody argued with an Aztec. Arguing with Aztecs made them angry. And an angry Aztec was awful and far from 'armless. In fact you'd be the arm-less one as they bit into your biceps.

Time was very important to the Maya — their gods controlled time, which in turn controlled the lives of humans. Here's how time ran out for the Indian nations. . .

Date	Mexico	Yucatan
3114 BC		The fifth age of humans begins. There have been four other human races before but the sun has destroyed them in turn as it will destroy this one!
1500 BC		The Mayan people change from hunting to farming; they begin to form into villages that all follow a similar way of life. (A bit like Millwall football supporters but not so vicious.)
1200 BC	In Eastern Mexico the Olmec people begin to take over . . . they use war clubs and punch with weapons attached to their fists. Sort of stone-age knuckle-	

300 BC

dusters! They sacrifice humans by clubbing them on the head. Olmecs disappear! They leave behind pyramids and stone carvings and the calendar.

200 BC

City of Teotihuacan is built in Mexico with pyramids and a main road known as the 'Avenue of the Dead'. It's at least two miles long. That's a lot of dead!

Mayan cities begin to grow with priests and kings having the power of life and death over the farming peasants.

AD 150

Start of the great age for Mexico. In Teotihuacan they offer human hearts to the gods. In 1,000 years the Aztecs will copy this idea!

The Maya begin to build temples which will grow bigger and richer in time.

WHAT DATE DO WE DISAPPEAR ON?

... AND OVER THERE IS THE 'STREET OF THE NOT VERY WELL'

MY TEMPLE'S BIGGER THAN YOUR TEMPLE

13

Date	Mexico	Yucatan
AD 300		Start of the great period of the Mayan people. Lots of great pyramid building and cruel ceremonies.
AD 600	Teotihuacan is destroyed. No one is sure why or who dunnit! Mexico filled with lots of tribes and cities.	
AD 850	Toltecs arrive in Mexico – great artists and builders. Pyramids as big as the ones in Egypt, and metal. End of Stone Age in Central America, but still they don't have the wheel!	The Mayan cities are abandoned. Why? Like the disappearance of dinosaurs, it's anybody's guess.

14

AD 1200 Now it's the turn of the Toltecs to be destroyed. They fall and their Tula City is ruined. Tribes from the north move into Mexico...

The Maya live on in small villages with a simple farming lifestyle.

WHAT'S SO SIMPLE ABOUT FARMING?

AD 1300 One of the last tribes to arrive are the Aztecs. They are fine fighters. Aztecs work as slaves for the people of Colhuacan, but murder the princess (in the hope that she'll become a war goddess). They are driven out and squeezed on to an island in a swamp ... but not for long.

SORRY WE'RE LATE

HOME SWAMP HOME

15

Date	Mexico	Yucatan
1345	The Aztecs build a new capital, Tenochtitlan (now Mexico City).	
1367	Aztecs fight for the Tepanec kingdom and go on to conquer the valley for them.	
1375	Aztecs decide it's time to elect a king to lead them.	
1427	Aztecs getting too powerful. Tepanec lords try to destroy them but the Aztecs fight back and become rulers of the valley.	
1492	Christopher Columbus lands in America. For Aztecs life will never be the same again. It will be worse.	

1519	Spanish conquistador Hernan Cortés lands in Mexico and Aztec King Motecuhzoma welcomes him as a god. But by ... Hernan Cortés has conquered the Aztecs. It takes him just 2 years.
1521	First Spanish trips into Mayan lands looking for gold. They don't find it, and Mayan warriors kill Spanish leaders ... but they'll be back!
1542	Spanish conquer most of the Maya, but tribes in the jungle will give trouble for centuries.
1696	Some of last free Mayan tribes meet Christian missionaries . . . and sacrifice them!
1901	Mexicans conquer the last free Mayan group. The Maya live on as peasants in the lands they used to rule.

THE MYSTERIOUS MAYA

Nations come and nations go. They can be a bit like balloons . . . they get bigger and bigger and bigger until suddenly . . . pop! They disappear quite suddenly.

The first great group of people in Central America were probably the Olmecs[1] – they started a lot of the ideas that the copy-cat Maya and Aztecs would take up later . . . courts for the fast and furious 'ball game', statues of gods and kings, pyramid temples . . . oh, and the nasty little habit of killing and eating people. (Well, nobody's perfect.) Then the Olmecs disappeared. Pop! (It would be nice to think they ate each other all up . . . but they probably didn't.)

IT READS: JUST POPPED OUT TO FIND SOMEONE TO EAT, BE BACK SOON

The Maya in Southern Mexico picked up where the Olmecs left off and built even bigger pyramids to sacrifice even more people. For over a thousand years they were the cleverest, most powerful people in the area. Then, in AD 900, their great cities with huge pyramids were abandoned. They were swallowed up for a hundred or more years by steamy jungle. Pop! At least, the cities went 'Pop!'. The Mayan people lived on as village farmers.

1. A few archaeologists are quite sure that the Maya came before the Olmecs. Some day they may prove it. But, even if the Maya did come first, it doesn't alter our story too much.

Further north in Mexico some of the strange Olmec and Mayan ways were being copied by the people of Teotihuacan (who went 'Pop!') then by the Toltecs (who went 'Pop!').

At last the Aztecs moved into the area, picked up a lot of Toltec ideas and habits and formed the last great people of Ancient Mexico. So, you see, if you want to understand the Aztecs you need to know a little about the Maya.

(And, by the way, the Aztecs didn't go mysteriously 'Pop!'. They were 'discovered' by people from Europe who came along and conquered them. But more of that later . . .)

The mystery of the Maya – 1

There are two mysteries. Where did the Maya come from? And where did the Maya go?

Where did they come from? They came from Asia, across to Alaska (when it was joined by a frozen sea) and down through what is now North America.[1]

Like their cave-cousins in Asia they made flint weapons and hunted animals. Then they began to settle down and grow food and build villages about 3,500 years ago.

They would pray to their gods that the rains would come and the crops would grow. After a few hundred years they

1. This happened 50,000 years ago or just 12,000 years ago depending on which archaeologists you believe! For you and me it doesn't matter.

found some people were better at praying than others. They made these people priests – which was nice for them because they didn't have to do all that hard work in the fields. While farmers farmed, the priests prayed and worked out a fantastic calendar so everyone would know when to sow their seeds and when to expect the rain.

This was a great success. If the rains came then the priests said, 'We told you we were good!' If the rains didn't come the priests said, 'You people must have been bad – the gods are annoyed – don't blame us!' Anyway, the priests became very popular and the farmers would take time off to build the priests bigger and better temples. They decided they'd be nearer heaven if they built them on high platforms.

In time (around 1,700 years ago) these platform temples became huge pyramids – then they built new pyramids round the old pyramids till they were as close to heaven as a pigeon on a pogo stick. The pyramids are deserted now but they are still there if you want to go and see them, trample over them and vandalize them the way tourists have for the past hundred years.

20

Hunters to farmers to priests. Simple, yes?
No.

Because some clever people came along, looked at the pyramids, looked at the native farmers and said, 'These simple farmers could never have built those pyramids!'

'So who did?' they asked themselves. (Clever people spend a lot of time talking to themselves.)

'The Egyptians built pyramids!' they answered themselves. 'The Egyptians must have sailed across the Atlantic Ocean 2,000 years before Columbus and settled in Mexico!'

Sensible historians said, 'This is all nonsense. Forget it. The Egyptians did not cross to South America.'

But on 1 September 1996 a sensational story appeared in the newspapers . . .

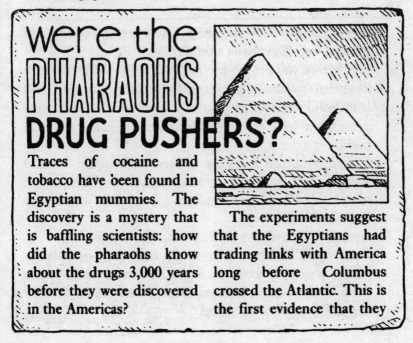

were the PHARAOHS DRUG PUSHERS?

Traces of cocaine and tobacco have been found in Egyptian mummies. The discovery is a mystery that is baffling scientists: how did the pharaohs know about the drugs 3,000 years before they were discovered in the Americas?

The experiments suggest that the Egyptians had trading links with America long before Columbus crossed the Atlantic. This is the first evidence that they smoked tobacco or chewed coca leaves – the source of cocaine.

German scientist Svetla Balabanova did not believe the results when she tested the mummies from British and German museums. 'The results were a shock. I was sure it was a mistake,' she said. But she was convinced after repeating the tests.

The Keeper of Egyptology at Manchester Museum said, 'We have always said there is no evidence of links between Egypt and the Americas – but there is never any evidence until it appears.'

The discovery of silk in the hair of 3,000-year-old mummies supports the claim that the pharaohs had trade links around the world. Cocaine has only been found in the coca plant in South America.

So there you are! A real mystery. There is just a chance that the Maya were Egyptians after all!

But before you get too excited look at the differences:

- Egyptian pyramids are carefully engineered and built from solid stone so they cover a tomb inside. They were graves, and took an incredible amount of brain-power to build.
- Mayan pyramids are piles of sand and rubble, covered with a stone face and an altar on the top. They were temple-platforms, and you didn't need to be a genius to build them.

Other writers have said the Mayan people were . . .

- Irish – the Irish are famous for their love of potatoes which originally grew in South America! Maybe they were early potato hunters who found their beloved vegetables and stayed there?

- Vikings – who, most historians agree, probably sailed to the north of America long before Columbus.
- Survivors from Noah's Ark – because Noah's Ark was built in America, some people say.

Y'ALL GO CHECK ON THEM THAR VARMITS Y'HEAR

- Survivors from the Greek defeat of Troy – who floated over the Atlantic on the wooden horse, perhaps?

YOU CAN LEAD A HORSE TO WATER BUT YOU CANNOT MAKE IT SINK

- Alexander the Great's Greek sailors – who turned right at the Mediterranean instead of left and became a little lost?
- Chinese – who turned left at Japan instead of right and crossed the Pacific by mistake?

There is, of course, one other explanation you might like to consider. In the 1960s a Swiss writer came up with a new theory. The beings who planned the Mayan pyramids weren't human. They were aliens from outer space! The pyramid platforms would make landing pads for their flying saucers! This may sound wacky and fantastic to you. But remember . . . he sold an awful lot of books!

Horrible habits

Whether the Maya came from the Mediterranean or Mars, the important question is, 'Would they be the sort of people you'd take home to meet your mum for tea?'

Here are some of their curious little habits . . .

Miserable Mayan children

Children in Mayan cities had a hard time. Maybe you'd prefer to be a Mayan rather than a modern?

1 In a Mayan city there were two wells. (Well, well!) One was for drinking and the other was for speaking to the gods. At dawn a girl would be thrown into the water almost 20 metres below. At noon she was brought out and asked, 'What did the gods say to you?' Whatever she replied the Maya would believe. (Of course there was a good chance that she'd have drowned. In that case she would not be saying very much. Oh, well.)

2 When a Mayan baby was born the child and its mother had to be ignored for three days. This was so evil spirits didn't notice there was a new body around to attack. The mother would tie cords around the baby's wrists and ankles to stop its soul escaping. Tied up and ignored – even a teacher shouldn't be treated like that . . . well, not tied up, anyway.

3 The Maya had broad heads. Broad heads were common

and the Mayan lords didn't want their children to look common. They wanted to give their children narrow heads. How do you narrow a child's head? Strap boards to either side as soon as the baby is born and keep them bound like that for at least two days. The poor babies would have to lie strapped in their cradles – board out of their minds.

4 Other heads were bound so that they were egg-shaped with the point at the back. Archaeologists have found these strange skulls and wonder how the owners could think straight. But they seemed to manage and the priests were clearly very clever people – real egg-heads in fact.

5 Cross-eyed kids are cute. Who says? The Maya. How do you make someone cross-eyed? Fasten a ball of wax to one of their head-boards (or to the hair on their forehead) and let it dangle in front of their noses. (If my parents did that to me then I'd be cross-eyed and how cross I'd be.)

6 The children were sent out to collect the nests of mud wasps. The nests were full of the maggots that would grow to become wasps. The mud nests were heated up until the

sweating maggots wriggled out. As soon as they did, the Maya would pop them into their mouths as a nice warm snack. (Try it some time. They'll give you more of a buzz than a packet of crisps.)

7 Boys would be taught to fish as soon as they were old enough. But the Maya cheated. They blocked off a stream with a dam then threw drugs into the water to knock out the fish. When the doped fish floated to the surface the Maya picked them out.

8 If a Mayan child died then its mother would cut the end off one of her own fingers and have it buried with the child! Pity the poor woman who lost ten children – still, she'd save on nail files.

9 Children were taught the importance of giving blood to the gods. If they couldn't sacrifice an enemy warrior then they could at least give some of their own blood. Blood was let out with the spines from a stingray's tail. In an important festival a Maya would give blood from the ears, the elbows and (if you were a boy) from your naughty bits! Oooof! Girls could instead pull a rope of thorns through a hole in their tongues. Owwww!

10 When a child was still very young it had its ears, its nose and its lips pierced so ornaments could be hung from them when it grew older. The wind must have whistled through all those holes like a bagpipe!

THAT SOUNDS LIKE SOMEONE'S TRYING TO PIERCE THE EARS OF A MAYAN *CAT*!

THANK YOU

It was a terrible crime for a Mayan man to run off with someone else's wife. If he was caught then the angry husband was allowed to kill the wife-stealer. He had to do this by dropping a rock on the victim's head!

Mayan lyin'

In the Ancient Mayan city of Chichen Itza there is a stone track over half a mile long. The track ends in a huge pit, 20 metres deep and filled with water.

A temple stands on the edge of the pit and owls are carved on the side of the temple. It is known as the Temple of the Owls (even your teacher could guess why).

There was an ancient story that said young girls were thrown to their deaths in the underground lake as sacrifices to the planet Venus. Nasty!

But when scientists dragged up dozens of human skeletons and examined them they found more than half were the bones of old people. (But don't get any ideas about throwing granny in the local swimming pool.)

So the story of sacrificing young girls was exaggerated. You can't believe everything you read . . . unless you read it in a Horrible Histories book, of course.

The story of the sacrifices at the Temple of the Owls was told on a wall painting at the temple. But tourists had a stupid sport of throwing bottles at the ancient painting. It is practically destroyed now. It's just a shame no one thought of throwing the tourists into the pit before they ruined the priceless painting for the rest of us!

April, Maya, June

The Maya created an incredible calendar that most of the nations of Central America copied for over a thousand years. They also had a form of picture writing (which other nations seemed to forget) and a system of numbers:

0	eye	7	·· — —	14	···· — — —
1	·	8	··· — —	15	— — —
2	··	9	···· — —	16	· — — —
3	···	10	— —	17	·· — — —
4	····	11	· — —	18	··· — — —
5	—	12	·· — —	19	···· — — —
6	· —	13	··· — —	20	eye

Amaze your friends by learning this system. It's easy really. The dot is one and the dash is five. So four dots is four, three dashes are fifteen. A dot and two dashes is eleven and so on. The sign for '0' is a shell.

28

Now you are a Mayan mathematician, can you spot which of the following sums is wrong?

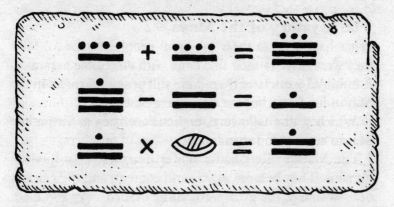

Years later the Aztecs were still using the bars and dot numbers to count how much people owed them! Why not use the system to claim a rise in pocket money? After all, it usually worked for the Aztecs (with a little help from a sacrificial altar, of course!).

Did you know . . . ?
The climate of the Mayan land is very damp and warm. Even in the dry season the air is heavy with moisture. This can be wonderful for plants to grow in but very tiring for visitors from Europe. And it can also cause other problems. An archaeologist working on a Mayan city site had continual problems with his ear. At last he reached a doctor

. . . and the doctor pulled out several tiny mushrooms that had taken root deep inside his ear!

The mystery of the Maya – 2

What happened to these powerful people? In the AD 900s they were there in their fine cities with incredible pyramids. A hundred years later there were still peasant farmers in the Mayan lands . . . but the cities were deserted.

Which of the following reasons have been given for the Mayan cities being abandoned?

1 The Mayan rulers had a slower heartbeat than modern humans. They became so lazy and content, and their hearts beat so slowly, the great lords simply faded away and died. With no leaders the people of the cities couldn't work together. The working farmers always worked harder and were fitter, so the peasants kept going.

2 The Maya didn't know about fertilizer. Their fields became too poor to grow the food the cities needed. The lack of food caused the city people to move away and find new land to farm.

3 There was a terrible earthquake. The people thought this was a punishment from the gods and fled from the danger of falling buildings. They never returned.

4 There was an invasion from northern Mexican tribes. The invaders robbed the rich and executed them or turned them into slaves.

5 The peasant farmers became fed up with the priests. The priests did no work but took large amounts of food as taxes. The farmers attacked the cities, wiped out the ruling classes and then returned to their fields.

6 There was a terrible plague. In Europe the Black Death left cities empty as people fled to find safety in the cleaner air of the countryside. Perhaps the Maya did the same but never returned.

> *Answer:* All of these ideas have been put forward. But they could all be wrong!
> Perhaps the rulers really were aliens who one day got homesick and flew back to Alpha Centauri. The simple natives couldn't run the cities without their alien lords!
> The truth is, no one really knows the answer. It's yet another mystery.

The Mayan gift

Whatever happened to the Ancient Maya it was probably what they deserved. Because they brought to Central America the horrible historical practice of human sacrifice. In order to keep the gods happy they would kill their prisoners of war. The peasant prisoners would be turned into slaves, but the lives of enemy leaders would make wonderful prezzies to the gods. (Imagine our dear Royal Family being the victims of an enemy sacrifice! You would miss them . . . wouldn't you?)

The sacrifice could be made anywhere but usually at a

temple pyramid and usually at a platform on the top of the pyramid.

The victims would be kept in cages while they waited to be sacrificed – some wall paintings in Mayan cities show these prisoners being tortured by having their fingernails torn out!

After ripping open the victim's chest and tearing the heart out, the victim was thrown down the side of the pyramid where priests were waiting to take the skin off and wear it to dance in.

Then bits of the victim were eaten. This was so that some of the spirit of the dead person could enter into the killers.

Imagine if this is true! Next time you eat a beefburger you could well become a real bull-y! If your mother feeds you pork chops then she can't complain if your room is like a pigsty. Chicken nuggets will turn you into a real bird brain, while fish and chips could help you win the next school swimming gala! Of course it sounds nonsense – 'Baa! Humbug!' as Mr Scrooge said when he finished his roast lamb with mint.

So, you see, the braver and more noble the victim, the braver and more noble the sacrificers became!

This Mayan religion was copied throughout Mexico and hundreds of thousands of people died. As late as 1696 the last free Mayan tribe disposed of some visiting missionaries by making them a ritual sacrifice.

Sort of, friar today, fried tomorrow.

Suffering slaves

Of course being a peasant prisoner wasn't much fun either. If you worked for an important person then there was a chance you'd be killed and buried so you could still serve your lord in the afterlife.

Long after the Mayan cities were abandoned, the idea of sending servants to the afterlife was still being copied.

Take the terrible Tarascans, for example. The Aztecs didn't conquer everyone in Central America. They didn't beat the tough Tarascan people for a start. The Tarascans were well organized and built strong fortresses that kept out the Aztec attackers.

They were also just as ruthless as the Aztecs. When their king died he was sent to the next life with all the people he'd need to run his palace there. The Tarascans executed and buried the following servants with the king . . .

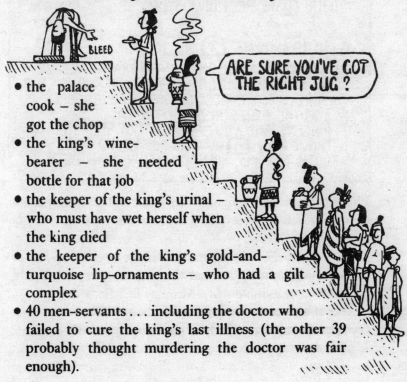

- the palace cook – she got the chop
- the king's wine-bearer – she needed bottle for that job
- the keeper of the king's urinal – who must have wet herself when the king died
- the keeper of the king's gold-and-turquoise lip-ornaments – who had a gilt complex
- 40 men-servants . . . including the doctor who failed to cure the king's last illness (the other 39 probably thought murdering the doctor was fair enough).

Dreadful dentists

Next time you have to go to the dentist you should be happy. It could be worse. You could have had a Mayan toothache. If you did then here's the cure . . .

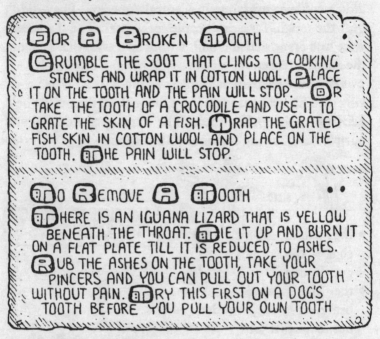

For a Broken Tooth

Crumble the soot that clings to cooking stones and wrap it in cotton wool. Place it on the tooth and the pain will stop. Or take the tooth of a crocodile and use it to grate the skin of a fish. Wrap the grated fish skin in cotton wool and place on the tooth. The pain will stop.

To Remove a Tooth

There is an iguana lizard that is yellow beneath the throat. Tie it up and burn it on a flat plate till it is reduced to ashes. Rub the ashes on the tooth, take your pincers and you can pull out your tooth without pain. Try this first on a dog's tooth before you pull your own tooth

The superstitious Maya believed that even dreaming about a broken tooth was a terrible curse – someone in the family would be sure to die.

They also believed that starting any job on a Tuesday or a Friday was unlucky . . . but the best time to plant seeds, get married or gamble was a Monday or a Saturday.

And the doctors weren't much better. They said that anyone who sneezes till their joints hurt will die within a day . . . unless you take a handful of orange leaves, boil them, rub the liquid into the feet and then all over the body! (Next time you sneeze you could try soaking your feet in orange squash. But don't pour it away and waste it. Take it to school the next day and give it to your worst enemy!)

Mayan medicine

Would you like to try any of the following tasty treats . . . even if you were dying?

1. EATING BIRD FAT

2. SMOKING TOBACCO (TO CURE SNAKE BITE!)

3. SWALLOWING RED WORMS

4. EATING BAT'S WINGS

5. DRINKING A WHOLE BAT DISSOLVED IN HONEY WINE

6. DRINKING A LIVE TOAD DISSOLVED IN WINE

7. SWALLOWING A WOODPECKER'S BEAK

8. EATING DRIED TAPIR DROPPINGS

9. EATING SHREDDED COCKEREL FEATHERS

'If all else fails,' one Mayan medical book says, 'have the sick person remove one sandal, urinate in it and drink it.'

The Maya did all of these things. So swallow your cod liver oil and stop complaining.

Did you know . . . ?
The Maya lived in an area to the south-east of Mexico that we call Yucatan.

But how did the place get its name? This is the true story!

The modern Maya
Since the destruction of the Mayan cities around AD 900, the Mayan people have survived in the south-east of Mexico. And they have had to survive some terrible tragedies in a horrible history.

When terrorists moved in to Mayan villages in the 1970s the poor villagers had to give them food and shelter. When the government fought back it was the Maya who received the worst of the punishments. Almost 200,000 were killed or 'disappeared'. Others fled and were forced to live in refugee camps in Mexico.

Mayan groups who stayed have seen their peasant farms destroyed and converted to huge cattle ranches to supply the Americans with beef for their hamburgers.

Maya who wanted to follow the old religions have been converted to Christianity . . . and, anyway, they can't go back to worship their old temples because they are swamped with tourists!

Still, the Maya are increasing in numbers and are hopeful. A new king will awaken in the ancient city of Chichen Itza, they say. He will rise along with thousands of warriors who have been frozen in time. A stone serpent with feathers will come to life and lead them all in a great war.

Perhaps those tourists had better take their cameras and run!

THE AWFUL AZTECS

The Aztecs (who called themselves the Mexica at first) probably lived in the north of Mexico until they decided to move south some time in the AD 1200s.

They said that they ate some fruit from the tree of a god. The god was so angry that he made the Aztecs wander through Central America. They must have arrived in the rich valley of Mexico in the early 1300s where the people living there called them 'the people whose face nobody knows'.

The wandering, homeless Aztecs were defeated and almost exterminated by the Lord of Culhuacan city. The surviving Aztecs became slaves. But even as slaves those Aztecs were a nuisance, so the Lord of Culhuacan sent them off to fight a powerful enemy who would finish them off . . . at least that's what he thought.

The Aztecs actually returned. The surprised Lord of Culhuacan said, 'You must have run away, you cowards!'

But the Aztec warriors opened sacks and poured out mountains of human ears over the lord's feet! 'These are from the enemy you sent us out to fight. We beat them!'

HELLO! WHAT HAVE WE EAR?

The story of the wandering is probably true – but what happened in the wanderings is most likely just Aztec legend. But there is something awfully, terribly possible about the legend of the Princess of Culhuacan . . .

The truth is the Aztecs would have learned about human heart sacrifices from the Toltecs themselves.

But why cut out human hearts and offer them to the gods? Where did this gruesome idea come from? The answer is that the Aztecs believed a legend from ancient Mexico and followed its teaching.

Imagine if we did that! If we actually believed a story like Hansel and Gretel and then acted as if it were true. Then every time we came across an old lady at her oven door we'd push her inside! It sounds crazy but that's why the Aztecs behaved the way they did. They believed that old story.

What was the story? Well, I'll tell you if you promise not to believe it and follow its lesson. Are you sitting comfortably? Then here it is . . .

The truly terrible tale

Once upon a time there were humans on the earth. And the humans ate maize and they grew into giants. (Now, cornflakes are made from maize. So, when your mother says, 'Eat up your cornflakes and you'll grow into a big strong person,' then you know she is telling the truth.)

But even these giants weren't tall enough to keep their heads above water when a great flood came. It swallowed the sun and ended the first age of the earth after 4,008 years. Almost every giant on earth was drowned and turned into a fish. That's where fish come from. (Remember that when you next eat fish fingers. You are really eating dead giants' fingers.)

Still, two humans survived by climbing into a tree. They were called Nene and Tata and they started the human race off all over again in the second age. But, after 4,010 years, what do you think happened? No, it wasn't another flood. This time there was a great wind that came along and blew out the sun.

The wind blew so hard that humans had to cling to the trees with their hands and feet and even grew tails. They all

41

turned into monkeys. That explains why the chimp in the local zoo looks so much like your Uncle Dave – they were both humans at one time . . . at least the chimp was.

Again, two humans survived by standing on a rock. They started the human race off all over again in the third age. But, after 4,081 years, what do you think happened? No it wasn't a flood and it wasn't a wind, it was a great fire that came along and destroyed the earth.

Of course, someone survived and started the fourth age and, of course, the humans of the fourth age were wiped out by rain of blood and fire. Nothing could grow and humans starved.

And that brings us to the fifth age – the one we're in now and the one that will end with earthquakes on 22 December 2012. (The Aztecs didn't have Christmas so they didn't realize how this will ruin everyone's Christmas in AD 2012. On the other hand you will be able to save money because there's no point in buying presents that will never get opened.)

At the start of the fifth age the gods met in Teotihuacan. That's a Mexican name that means 'The place where the gods are born'.

And it was dark. (Well, it would be, since the sun of the fourth age had been destroyed by the rain of blood and fire.) As you may know, there is only one way to make a sun, and that is for a god to set fire to himself.

Nobody wanted the job. Would you?

At last the boastful Tecuciztecatl said he was the greatest god and he really should be the new sun. No one agreed because no one really liked him. Still they built a huge bonfire and invited Tecuciztecatl to jump in.

The god looked at the fire and suddenly remembered he

was far too busy to become the sun today. Tecuciztecatl was Tecucizte-totally-chicken. That's when the wise and popular Nanahuatzin took a long run, a hop, a step and a jump and landed in the fire. Pow! The earth had a sun.

Tecuciztecatl was so ashamed of himself he too took a long run, a jump, a step and a hop and followed Nanahuatzin. Pow! The earth had another great ball of light in the sky – Tecuciztecatl had become the moon.

The gods were feeling pretty pleased with themselves when one of them pointed to the sun in the sky and said, 'It isn't moving!'

And it was true. Nanahuatzin had given his life to make the sun, now he wanted the other gods to give their lives before he would set off across the sky.

Of course they grumbled a bit at first. 'I wish he'd said that before he jumped in the fire,' one of them muttered.

'Well, it's done now,' another one said reasonably. 'I'll give my heart if you'll give yours!'

So, one by one, the gods came to the feathered snake god, Quetzalcoatl, and had their living hearts torn out of their bodies. When the sacrifices had been made the sun began to move across the sky as it has done ever since.

It was said giants built the pyramids of the sun and of the moon in Teotihuacan and the first leaders were buried inside them. The ruins of the pyramids still stood in Teotihuacan when the first Aztecs arrived in Mexico. The simple Aztecs looked at the pyramids, were sure they could only have been built by giants and they really believed the tale of the gods.

BUT . . . the Aztecs said, 'If the gods had to give their hearts to keep the sun moving in the sky then we humans should do the same. We must make sure the sun is properly fed with regular supplies of heart.'

And that's why the Aztecs began sacrificing humans to the gods.

It's silly and it's savage and thousands of people died horrible deaths, all because of a story.

Did you know . . . ?
A Spanish priest called Siguenza came to Mexico in the 1500s. He didn't believe the story about the gods of Teotihuacan. But he didn't believe that normal humans had built those great pyramids in the deserted city either. He had a different theory about the people who built the pyramids. He said some incredible people had arrived in Mexico from a huge island called Atlantis before it sank into the sea. And even to this day some people believe that's where the ancient Mexican rulers came from.

Swamp serpent soup

The greatest Aztec legend says they were led to their new land by a prophet called Tenoch. If the first settlers had written letters back to their old homeland then they may have looked something like this . . .

Dear Mum

Here we are in our new home and it's really smashing. Lots to eat. As you know, Tenoch the prophet led us down here from Aztlan and kept going on about a snake and an eagle and a cactus. He'd had a dream. Well, we all have dreams but we don't go rushing off with half the tribe to make the dreams come true, do we? Personally, Mum, I thought he was potty. But we pushed on until we reached this swampy lake. A horrible place, but the land around the lake was fine.

Of course the trouble was - you've guessed it - some other tribes already live on this land. Now I'm a warrior, as you know, Mum, but their warriors were bigger than me and there were more of them. "What do we do, Tenoch?" we asked.

"We talk," he said. "We ask them to give us some land."

If I thought Tenoch was a nutter <u>before</u> then I was <u>sure</u> he was a few bricks short of an adobe then! Ask! For land!

Anyway, we asked. The five tribes were ready with an answer. They had smug little grins on their ugly little faces as they pointed at the lake. Because there, in the middle of the lake, was an island. They even offered Tenoch a boat to go and have a look at it. So off he paddled and came back a while later. "The snake, the eagle and the cactus!" he cried. "It is my dream! I saw an eagle, perched on a cactus tearing at a snake it had caught!"

"Oh, yes, didn't we tell you?" the enemy chief said. "The island is full of snakes! Poisonous snakes!" he chuckled. That's when I saw their sneaky little plan! They wanted rid of us so they sent us across to a snake-infested island so the serpents could kill us off.

They don't know the Aztecs! We jumped into the boats and paddled there as fast as the weeds would let us!

We jumped ashore and were met by the snakes. Lovely, long fat things. And they'd never seen many humans before. They just looked at us with their cute little faces and licked their poisonous fangs with their pretty purple tongues. There was a funny sort of surprised expression on their faces as their heads hit the ground.

The snakes were as simple as the tribes-folk. They didn't know that a favourite Aztec meal is snake meat!

'**S**o I can't wait for you to come and join us, Mum. Snake soup, snake stew, roast snake steak, minced snake burgers and spicy snake fry. I'm working on a new recipe myself. I call it snake and kidney pie.

So we've named our new home Tenochtitlan, after the prophet. Still, I have a feeling we won't be staying here for long. Those smug little tribes had better watch out. We weren't killed off by the snakes. We are warriors and we'll be looking for someone to war against very soon.

Your loving son,

Mex

The Aztecs soon turned the shallow lake into *chinampas* – gardens made by piling up mud from the bottom of the lake. They built bridges and canals for transport and soon became a great trading centre. They also set about seizing power from the surrounding tribes.

The Aztecs proved to be fierce and fearless fighters.

By 1520 the Aztec emperor Motecuhzoma II ruled over a great empire in Central America. Little did he know that

47

the Spanish were coming and the mighty Aztecs were going to fall a lot quicker than they had risen.

It's easy to think the Aztecs arrived with their special way of life and they forced the rest of Mexico to follow them. But things don't work like that. The Aztecs took control of the Toltec lands – but the Toltec religion took control of the Aztec minds!

And the Toltecs had been very bloodthirsty people. Very, very. In fact you could say very, very, VERY!

The good gore guide

You know that the sun is a star . . . a large celestial body composed of gravitationally contained hot gases emitting electromagnetic radiation, especially light, as a result of nuclear reactions inside the star. (No, I don't understand what it means either but it sounds good if you say it quickly.)

Anyway, the Toltecs believed it was actually a god. A superhuman being who has power over human life.

Now these god people can be very tricky. If you upset them then they'll make you suffer – shine too hot on your crops, shrivel them up and starve you, or send a plague of locusts to eat all your food. The thing to do is keep your god (or gods) happy.

Some people think their god will be happy with a bit of praise and a few hymns and prayers. Other people believe they have to give prezzies to their god.

The terrible Toltecs believed you had to give a life to their god – a sacrifice.

But the awful Aztecs took it to extremes. They believed they had to give their sun god human lives – thousands of them. And, not only that, they had to be sacrificed in a gruesomely gory way.

HEALTH WARNING: Readers who are sickened at the sight of a squashed rabbit on the road should NOT read this section.

The Aztecs didn't sacrifice the odd human on special occasions like the king's birthday or Bank Holiday Mondays. They did it all the time. They . . .

- sacrificed 50,000 a year (that's a thousand a week, six an hour or one every ten minutes!)
- sacrificed 20,000 in a single party when they opened the temple at Tenochtitlan
- had an army specially organized to keep the priests supplied with victims
- stirred up trouble among the conquered tribes so they had an excuse to go in and take prisoners who became sacrifice victims.

A Spanish history book said that when the Great Temple was opened in 1487 there were 80,000 victims sacrificed in one ceremony. But don't believe everything you read in history books! Because sacrificing 80,000 would have been just about impossible! The Aztecs would have needed machine guns and bombs to massacre that many. (In fact it's only in the past hundred years that humans have learned to kill each other at that rate – but modern people call it war and that makes it all right.)

What a way to go...
The Aztecs preferred sacrificing enemy warriors. The braver the enemy then the better the sacrifice. If an Aztec captured an enemy he would say, 'Here is my well-beloved son.' The victim would reply, 'Here is my dearest father.' You might say this sort of thing when you're asking for more pocket money! You'd better hope 'dearest' father doesn't then go on to sacrifice you.

The Aztecs had five main ways of sacrificing their victims – some more cruel than others. Which would you choose? Here's a rough guide. How would you score the methods?

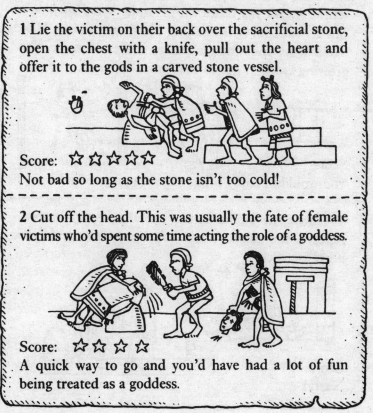

1 Lie the victim on their back over the sacrificial stone, open the chest with a knife, pull out the heart and offer it to the gods in a carved stone vessel.

Score: ☆☆☆☆☆
Not bad so long as the stone isn't too cold!

2 Cut off the head. This was usually the fate of female victims who'd spent some time acting the role of a goddess.

Score: ☆☆☆☆
A quick way to go and you'd have had a lot of fun being treated as a goddess.

3 Tie the victim to a large rock and give him a sword club to defend himself. He then fights against an Aztec warrior whose sword club has a knife edge.

Score: ☆ ☆ ☆
You'd go down fighting but you wouldn't last long!

4 Tie the victim to poles and fill him full of darts or arrows. Mark his heart with a white spot, but don't aim at that spot with the first few dozen arrows. The blood from the wounds makes the earth richer for growing crops . . . or so the Aztecs believed.

Score: ☆ ☆
You wouldn't enjoy being a human pin-cushion.

5 Throw the victim into a fire then pull him out, repeat a few times. When he's lightly baked, do the heart sacrifice.

Score: ☆
Nasty!

Monster mother

In 1803 Baron Friedrich Heinrich Alexander von Humboldt visited Mexico to study Aztec history. He uncovered a 3-metre high statue that weighed 12 tons. It had been carved out of a single block of volcanic stone and it was horrible. In fact it was so shocking that he buried it again!

It was a statue of the goddess Coatlicue. Victims were sacrificed in front of Coatlicue . . . and after seeing her ugliness they might have died of the shock before the priests got them!

Cuddly Coatlicue was roughly human in shape but had . . .

- a double head of two snakes facing one another
- snakes for arms
- a cloak of snakes twisted in the wings of a vulture
- feet of a jaguar (the big cat, not the car, stupid)
- a necklace of hearts, skulls and severed hands strung together with guts.

Do you ever get bored in your school art lessons? Why not ask teacher if you can make a model of Coatlicue from modelling clay? (You don't get ideas like this on *Blue Peter*.)

When it's finished you can rip out the living heart of a jelly baby as a sacrifice. (Use a spoon for this because we wouldn't want you to cut yourself, would we?)

There is every chance that if you follow these instructions you will be expelled from your school, for being sick and disgusting. So that's another reason for doing it!

Here is cool, cute and blood-curdling Coatlicue.

SSSSSS

Remind you of anyone?

Coatlicue's story is as gruesome as her statue. Coatlicue was a goddess and was expecting the baby who would grow up to be the sun. But before the baby was born Coatlicue was murdered by her daughter, the goddess of the moon, and her 400 sons who were the stars. They cut off Coatlicue's head – and the snakes from the neck are an image of the blood gushing out.

But the baby was born anyway and he avenged his mother's death by throwing the moon goddess off a mountain and defeating his 400 brothers. (What a baby!)

Every dawn the sun drives the moon and stars from the sky – provided he gets his regular supply of sacrifice blood, of course.

It's certain that some sacrifices ended with some bits of some victims being cooked and eaten. (The arms and the thighs were the only bits the priests allowed people to eat.) In the 1980s clever professors reckoned that the Aztecs had huge cannibal feasts – all that meat gave them the strength to fight and capture even more victims.

In the 1990s even cleverer professors say this idea is potty.

In fact the Aztecs had plenty to eat without picnicking on people . . .

EAT LIKE AN AZTEC

Funny food

It's hard to imagine modern food without the plants discovered in Mexico 500 years ago. For example, the Maya gave us chicle – for chewing gum. And the Aztecs had other treats. What would your life be like without. . .

- spices . . . like chilli pepper for curry
- corn . . . to make your cornflakes
- pumpkin . . . so Cinderella could get to the ball and you can have a hallowe'en lantern
- tomatoes . . . for the sauce in your baked beans
- turkeys . . . for your Christmas dinner.

The Aztecs had chocolate beans but they were so precious they were used as money. They grew peanuts that traders brought from South America. Imagine the cinema without the Aztecs – no popcorn or peanuts or chocolates.

Of course, the Mexicans didn't have cooking fat before the Spanish arrived with pigs from Europe. The Aztecs had never tasted fried food. So a great invention like chips needed potatoes (which originally came from South America) to get together with European frying before it could be enjoyed.

Ten tasty treats you wouldn't want to eat...

The people of Mexico have always had interesting food. 10,000 years ago they were driving mammoths into swamps and killing them with stone knives and spears. They would make real jumbo meals.

We can enjoy a lot of pleasant food thanks to the people of Mexico. But there are some things they used to eat that you may not be so keen to taste. Things like . . .

1 Monkeys – the spider monkey and the howler monkey were enjoyed by the Aztecs and are still eaten by the native inhabitants today! The howler monkey gets its name from its roar that can be heard at least 3 km (2 miles) away. If we could understand them they'd probably be howling, 'Look out! The Aztecs are coming to eat you!'

2 Toads – archaeologists found bones from marine toads in many early Mexican villages. Since the skins of these toads are poisonous they guess that they were used as a sort of drug, but too much could kill you. Wart a way to go!

3 Frogs – are safer than toads and very tasty – ask any French chef. And the Aztecs could crack awful jokes like:

4 Cactus – the maguey cactus was amazingly useful. The Aztecs used it to make needles (and the spikes) and thread, and as fuel, from paper, rope, cloth, mats and as thatching for their house roofs. The plant was boiled to give a sweet syrup and the syrup could be used to make a sort of cactus wine. The trouble was there was an Aztec law against getting drunk and the punishment was death.

5 Dogs – that's right. You wouldn't want pet pie, baked beagles on toast, Yorkshire terrier pudding or a boxer chocolate would you? Would you wolf hound after you whippet out of the oven? Surely not. The Aztecs would.

6 Lake scum – yes, the green stuff you see floating on top of the park pond. The Aztecs in Teotihuacan would collect it from the edge of the lake, press it into cakes and eat it. The trouble was the lake became polluted with chemicals used to make whitewash for the houses. Some of this scum could make an Aztec sick as a Panama parrot.

7 Lizards – tricky to catch but a very tasty bit of meat on the creatures. Nothing better than a lizard in your gizzard . . . it's wizard!

8 Ants – people in Europe are used to being eaten by ants when they try to picnic in a field. But the Aztecs had a better idea . . . they ate the ants. Lovely crunchy little snacks! Would you eat one? Perhaps one crawled into your picnic sandwich when you weren't looking!

Perhaps you've already become an Aztec ant-eater!

9 Tadpoles – ask your parents about sago. It's a sort of rice-pudding dish but with clear globules that look like frogspawn. It was served regularly for school dinners – and refused regularly by children. The Aztecs would have enjoyed it because they ate tadpoles.

10 Larvae – you know what they are? Insects before they grow up. So fly larvae are known as maggots and butterfly larvae are caterpillars while beetle larvae are known as grubs.

THOSE AZTECS CERTAINLY KNOW HOW TO ENJOY THEIR GRUB!

Something you wouldn't want to drink . . .
The Mayans learned to make strong alcohol from the runny honey of their bees. But the honey needed bacteria (germs) to make it turn into alcohol. How did they put the germs into the honey?

Answer: Girls took the honey into their mouths, swished it round and they all spat it out into a large bowl. After a few days it began to froth and bubble and turn into alcohol.
But don't try this at home . . . all that honey-swishing will make your teeth rot!

. . . and what the Aztecs didn't want to eat
Surprisingly, they didn't want to eat chocolate. The Aztecs had cacao beans from which we now make chocolate. They

knew how to grind up these beans, boil them to a froth with water and sweeten the drink with vanilla and honey.

So why didn't the Aztecs drink this tasty stuff?

Because the cacao beans were too precious. For an Aztec, making a cup of chocolate would be like you eating a five-pound note sandwich . . . a waste of money.

Of course rich people liked to show off by drinking chocolate. They could afford it.

Food you might like to eat

Tortillas

The main food of the Aztecs would be maize which they ate with almost everything. They would make very thin maize 'pancakes', called tortillas, and use them to scoop up food

from a dish or to make a parcel around some filling.

Maize flour is not common outside of Mexico but ordinary flour would do. You can make about 6 tortillas with 150g of plain flour, 25g of lard and 90ml of warm water. Mix it into a dough and roll it so thin you can see the board underneath. Then heat a 20-25cm circle of dough on a flat-bottomed frying pan for about 40 seconds. It should bubble if the temperature is right. (Well, you'd bubble if you were thrown into a hot pan, wouldn't you?) Turn it over and cook the other side for about 30 seconds.

Best of all is to buy your tortillas ready-made from a supermarket!

Quesadillas

Heat a heavy frying pan till sprinkled water sizzles on it. Drop a tortilla on to the hot pan. Cover the tortilla with about 25g of grated cheese then some thin slices of onion. Lastly pop another tortilla on top. After about a minute or two the cheese begins to melt. Turn the whole thing over and heat for another minute. Eat!

You can add strips of sliced green chilli if you want a flavour of the Aztecs' favourite spice.

Burritos

The people of the USA call tortilla snacks 'burritos'. That means 'little donkeys' . . . but don't worry, they don't have to take nuggets of Neddy from the knackers' yard. There is no donkey-meat in this at all. They are fillings of whatever you fancy wrapped in tortilla parcels.

It's a dog's life

Mexican dogs probably had very happy lives. They would not have been so happy if they knew what was going to happen to them! Luckily dogs can't see into their future. So, if you have a dog, be kind to it – don't tell it about Aztec dogs and don't leave this book lying around where Rover can read it. Because . . .

- The Aztecs bred small dogs for food. These dogs were practically hairless because it was so warm in Mexico . . . in fact they were dogs with no ruff at all. These dogs were pot-bellied little things and Mexican potters were so fond of them they made clay models of the cute curs.

- The Maya bred dogs that didn't bark! That would give them a bit of peace and quiet at night . . . but how did the poor mutts talk to one another?

- Some natives of Mexico believed a dog could help its owner to cross over into the afterlife when they died. The trouble was the dog had to be dead at the time. Whenever an owner died then the dog would be killed and buried with them. Sort of 'Spot!' Splatt!

AZTEC DAYS

Disgusting Diary

The Aztecs had a calendar of 365 days – like us but without the leap years. This calendar, and the movement of the stars and the sun, gave them a disgusting diary for the years.

The city of Tenochtitlan was massive and the twin pyramids of the Great Temple looked down on the streets. Twin pyramids to the gods – the gods of life and the gods of death . . . but mainly death for the people who were conquered by the Aztec warriors.

And the streets below weren't filled with filth and rotting rubbish like the streets of Europe at that time. They were kept clean by thousands of sweepers every day. Rubbish was collected, loaded on to barges and shipped away to be dumped.

The sweepers were usually captives from other tribes who were forced to serve the Aztecs. If one of those sweepers had kept a diary then it would have been gruesome. It may have looked something like this. . .

⓫ NOVEMBER – ⓴ NOVEMBER : DAYS OF THE PRECIOUS FEATHER

⓫ NOVEMBER New Year. And how do the warriors celebrate? They fast – starve themselves for days on end. I'm glad I'm not a warrior who has to fast . . . it's bad enough being a slave. I've had my breakfast, but I'm still so hungry I could eat three dogs and still find room for a rattlesnake.

---

⑮ NOVEMBER Today the Aztecs remember the dead warriors. Well, the older warriors remember them. I would have remembered them but I forgot. Great hunting with prizes for the best hunters. Because this is the time of the hunter they take their prisoners, tie them up like deer, their front legs to their back legs. (Yes, I know people don't have front legs, but they pretend.) Then the priests sacrifice them like deer – which they are really. You hear them moaning, 'Oh, deer! Oh, deer! Oh deer!' There's a lot of mess to clear up, of course. Still. It could be worse. It could be me they're sacrificing!

⓲ NOVEMBER This is the 'eating of the water tamales' day. They only have this once every eight years . . . thank the gods! The Aztecs only eat water-soaked tamales – meat and maize flour – no spices so it's like a tasteless mush. Up at the temple there are some very nice dances but the Aztecs have to go and spoil it, don't they? They end with a ceremony where they swallow water-snakes and frogs. It makes you hungry just watching them. I prefer my snake-meat roasted.

🔢 NOVEMBER – 🔟 DECEMBER : DAYS OF THE RAISING OF BANNERS

🔢 NOVEMBER The Aztecs celebrate the birthday of Huitzilopochtli, who grew up to beat Coyolxauhqui in battle. People wave paper flags from the houses and hang them from fruit trees! Everyone enjoys themselves ... except the prisoners who get sacrificed at the Great Pyramid of Tenochtitlan. They don't complain for long.

🔢 DECEMBER – 🔢 DECEMBER : DAYS OF THE DESCENT OF WATER

🔢 DECEMBER It's wet. That's why they call these days the 'Days of the Descent of Water', because it usually rains about this time. Well, at least it's giving the pyramid a good wash down. But it's cold and muddy work out on the streets. At least it's a quiet time for the sacrifices. None of the nasty bits to sweep up.

🔢 DECEMBER – 🔢 JANUARY : DAYS OF THE STRETCHING

🔢 JANUARY The merchants pray for good trade. They sacrifice a few slaves, of course. And the priests dress up as gods and do some very nice dancing before a great feast with the lords. Of course, I never get invited to the feasts. Remind me never to become a merchant slave. I really don't want my heart ripped out of my chest – even if the Aztecs say it is a great honour.

㉖ JANUARY Today's the day they grab the children and pull them by the neck to make them grow. Mum used to do it to me. It didn't half hurt. Still, I'm nice and tall – I've a neck like a rattlesnake, but I'm nice and tall. I held my little brother's legs while Mum pulled his head. You should have heard the neck-bones creak!

㉘ JANUARY Today the children have their ears pierced. At least, the children who survived the neck-stretching have their ears pierced! I held my little brother down while our mum drilled the holes. He didn't half squawk.

㉛ JANUARY The Aztecs honour the fire god today. Toast corn in front of his altar and toast a few animals too. Of course it's the priests who get to eat these gifts to the god. I wonder if the god ever gets hungry himself? Lots of sweeping up after ceremonies like this.

🟸 FEBRUARY - 🟸 FEBRUARY: THE USELESS DAYS

🟸 FEBRUARY The Aztecs have 18 months of 20 days each in their calendar. So they have these five 'useless days' left over. Everybody says they're really unlucky. (Of course no one gets sacrificed in the useless days, so I guess slaves and prisoners think they're really useful days!) And no one does any work on these days. I decided it would be best to stay in bed so the bad luck couldn't get me. But I fell out of bed. It didn't half hurt!

🟸 FEBRUARY - 🟸 MARCH: THE RAISING OF THE TREES DAYS

🟸 FEBRUARY They don't really raise trees, of course. They raise poles with banners on them, then they make sacrifices to the gods of the maize and the rain. This time they sacrifice children, but at least they take them up to the mountains to sacrifice them. Less mess for me to clean up. They say the more the children cry the happier the rain god will be. If it was me I'd squawk like a parrot.

🟸 MARCH - 🟸 MARCH: THE FLAYING OF MEN DAYS

🟸 MARCH The young warriors have mock battles. Very entertaining and not too messy. But the priests make the usual sacrifices and wear the skins of the victims. I wouldn't be seen dead in a cloak of human skin myself. These Aztecs have very bad taste and they expect us slaves to clean up after them. It's a dog's life at times. (Except, of course, slaves don't get eaten like

68

the dogs!) At least they put the skins in a holy cave in the temple. Makes a change to have priests clearing up after themselves, I can tell you. They wear those skins for 20 days. My friend cleans at the temple and says they smell dreadful!

26 MARCH – 14 APRIL : THE OFFERING OF FLOWERS DAYS

3 APRIL Spring's here so the Aztecs go into the fields to sacrifice flowers! I was sweeping between the pyramids of the Great Temple today when a priest came out. He explained that the pyramids are like life and death. 'Life needs death to exist; and death needs life,' he said. I just nodded and hoped he didn't want *my* life! The blood doesn't half dye the steps up to the top of the pyramids. I could scrub for days and never get those stains out. I'm glad that's not my job.

15 APRIL – 4 MAY : DAYS OF THE GREAT VIGIL

3 MAY Young Aztec girls go in procession to bless the maize in the fields. I don't get to go, of course. More children sacrificed on the mountains. It makes you wonder how there's any children left the rate these Aztecs sacrifice them!

🄯 MAY – 🄯 MAY: DAYS OF DRYNESS

🄯 MAY It's dry. The dust in the streets is terrible and I get home filthy every night. The priests have a young man who pretends to be the god Tezcatlipoca. He has a wonderful time, him being treated like a god and all that. The trouble is gods don't get old, so they have to have a new young man every year. What happens to the old one? He gets sacrificed, of course.

🄯 MAY – 🄯 JUNE : DAYS OF EATING MAIZE AND BEANS

🄯 JUNE The end of the dry season and all that mud again. They give offerings of foods to the tools they use in the fields! I wish they'd offer some to me. They bring reeds from the lakes to make new mats, seats and decorations for the temples. There's bits of reed all over the place. Sweeping up reeds in mud isn't easy.

🄯 JUNE – 🄯 JULY: DAYS OF THE FEASTS OF THE LORDS

🄯 JUNE The lord of Tenochtitlan invites the common people to some great feasts. Of course the common Aztecs go but the slaves like me just get the job of clearing up after them. Still, there's always food left over so for once I can't complain.

24 JULY – 11 SEPTEMBER: DAYS OF THE FEAST OF THE DEAD

13 SEPTEMBER Feasts, feasts, feasts. Any excuse. Now they're honouring the dead. These Aztecs have a good life. Apart from the sacrifices today they had this brilliant pole-climbing contest. My mum told my little brother to be careful not to win. It doesn't do to get yourself noticed. Not if you want to stay alive in Tenochtitlan!

12 SEPTEMBER – 11 OCTOBER: DAYS OF THE SWEEPING

11 OCTOBER The Aztecs have a good old clean out. And where does their rubbish end up? On the streets. And who gets the job of clearing it? Me and the other sweepers. This is the time of the year when the gods return to the temples for the winter. At midnight last night the first god arrived and showed he was there by leaving a footprint in a bowl of flour in the temple. It's flour made out of maize and my mum says it's an a-maize-ing trick. She can be funny, my mum.

12 OCTOBER – 31 OCTOBER: DAYS OF THE FEAST OF THE MOUNTAINS

31 OCTOBER Those Aztecs have a plant called amaranth. Today they ground it up into a paste and baked it into models of the gods and snakes. But did they eat them? No! They offered them to the gods. I'll never understand these Aztecs if I live to be 50 years old. In fact I would be glad to reach 15 years old! I'm just grateful I've survived another year without getting myself sacrificed.

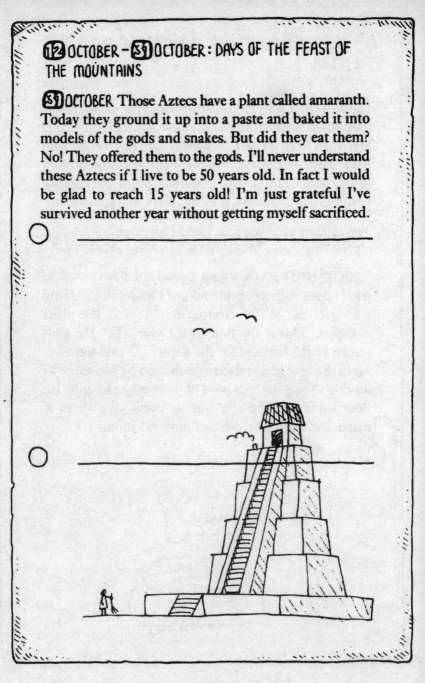

LIVE LIKE AN AZTEC

The Aztecs were fighters. By 1500 they had conquered most of Mexico. The defeated people had to supply the Aztec homeland at Tenochtitlan with food, clothing and slaves.

But most of all the Aztecs wanted defeated warriors for their sacrifices.

Problem: How could they defeat warriors when they'd conquered Mexico and there was no one left to beat?

Answer: The Aztecs sent in spies. Aztec traders went in disguise to strange cities and looked for signs of rebellion against the Aztec rule. If they found any sign of rebel forces they encouraged it! 'Go on . . . fight the Aztecs! I'll bet you could beat the loincloths off them, lads!'

As soon as the rebels went into action the Aztecs would attack and win. They would win because their trader-spies would have told them all the enemy weaknesses.

THEY ALWAYS STOP FOR TEA AT FOUR O'CLOCK

The Aztec warriors tried to capture the rebels alive so they could sacrifice them later in Tenochtitlan. That's mean and that's cheating . . . but it was the Aztec way of making sure the sun kept moving in the sky.

73

Cruel to kids

If you wanted the gods to bring you rain or a good harvest then you had to give them gifts. You had to give them really precious gifts, of course, not just any old rubbish. What was the most precious gift they could give? A life. And what was the most precious life? The life of a child, of course. The Aztecs must have really loved children because they sacrificed dozens every year.

Of course these would usually be captured slave children. Aztecs were a bit tougher with their own children. The Aztec child was taught not to expect a happy life . . . and it didn't get one! How would you like to have been an Aztec child?

THE GOOD AZTEC PARENT IS STRICT. THEN THEIR CHILD WILL GROW UP TO BE HARD-WORKING AND OBEDIENT. A USEFUL AZTEC ADULT.

FROM THE AGE OF 4 GIRLS WILL COOK AND CLEAN WHILE BOYS WILL GO FISHING OR WORKING IN THE FIELDS

THE DISOBEDIENT CHILD MAY BE PINCHED ON THE ARMS OR THE EARS

THE REALLY DISOBEDIENT CHILD MAY BE PRICKED WITH THE THORNS FROM THE MAGUEY CACTUS

Did you know . . . ?

1 Boys were trained to be warriors. When they were baptized at a few days old they were given their warrior equipment – a miniature loincloth, a cloak, a shield and four arrows.

2 As boys grew older they were told, 'The house you were born in is not your true home – that is out there on the battlefield. Your mission is to give the sun the blood of your enemies to drink.'

3 Girls, on the other hand, were given a skirt, a blouse and weaving equipment. They were told that their place was in the home.

4 The first words a baby heard when it was born were: 'You have come to this earth which is a place of torment, a place of pain, a place of weariness, a place of illness, thirst, hunger and weeping.' Cheerful stuff. Just the sort of thing you want to hear after all the effort to get born in the first place.

5 A child would be named after the day on which it was born. There were 20 days and 18 months but the months could have some embarrassing names. Imagine going through life as Six Dog (you'd be sick as a dog), Ten Crocodile (you'd be a bit snappy), or Eight Monkey (and if you were Aztec you would have ate monkey). Perhaps you'd prefer to be a Wind, a Vulture, a Rabbit, a Lizard, a Flower or a Death's Head?

6 Pottery figures of around AD 600 to 900 show Mexican native boys grinning . . . with their top teeth filed to a point! It probably helped them eat their roast dog. But would you like to have your teeth filed? Eeeeugh!

DO YOU HAVE ANY FILLINGS?

NOPE, BUT I'VE GOT A COUPLE OF FILINGS

7 If a family was very poor then there was a quick and easy way to make some money. Sell the kids! This was an idea copied from the Maya. Slave traders would buy healthy children and take them to market. The children would have to work hard for hours on end or be punished. A bit like school, really.

HOW MANY TIMES DO I HAVE TO TELL YOU, WE AREN'T POOR, WE DON'T HAVE TO SELL YOUR LITTLE BROTHER

8 If a child died then it wouldn't get a coffin. It would be buried in a jar. Hopefully no one would later dig up the jar and mistake it for a jar of jam.

9 The Aztecs were certainly the only people in the world of the 1500s to have schooling for all boys and girls. But they didn't start school till they were 15 years old and stopped at the age of marriage – about 20. The boys could choose between schools for priests and schools for warriors. Girls generally learned singing and dancing. Then, of course, there was . . .

Mexican marriage

Want to marry your loved one in a genuine Aztec ceremony? This is how boys can go about it. (Sadly, girls, you don't have a lot of say in this!)

Could you survive as an Aztec? Imagine you are an Aztec boy. Try the following test.

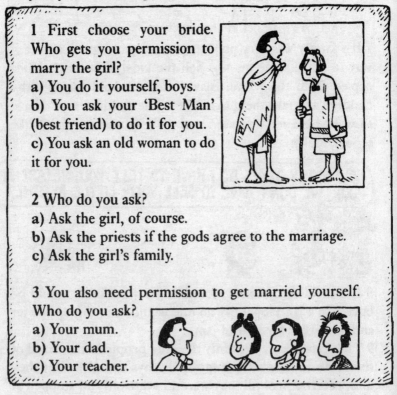

1 First choose your bride. Who gets you permission to marry the girl?
a) You do it yourself, boys.
b) You ask your 'Best Man' (best friend) to do it for you.
c) You ask an old woman to do it for you.

2 Who do you ask?
a) Ask the girl, of course.
b) Ask the priests if the gods agree to the marriage.
c) Ask the girl's family.

3 You also need permission to get married yourself. Who do you ask?
a) Your mum.
b) Your dad.
c) Your teacher.

4 How do you choose your wedding day?
a) You agree a day with your bride.
b) Everyone marries on the same day so you don't have to choose.
c) Read your horoscope and make sure it is a 'good' day on the Aztec calendar.

5 There is a feast before the wedding. Who arranges that?
a) You do it yourself, cooking food that you've hunted for yourself.
b) Your mother cooks your favourite meal with enough for everyone to share.
c) The bride's parents arrange the feast so you don't have to worry about a thing.

6 The wedding takes place after the feast and at night. How does the bride travel to your house for the ceremony?
a) In a taxi.
b) You carry her on your back.
c) She is carried on the back of an old woman.

7 How do the guests get from the feast to the wedding at your house?

79

a) They ride on the backs of oxen.

b) They form a long line, join hands and dance from the bride's house to yours.

c) They have a torch-lit procession.

8 Everyone gives you a wedding present. When do you get your presents?

a) When you move into your new house.

b) Straight after the wedding.

c) Just before the wedding.

9 How are you joined together in marriage?

a) You and your bride each grip one end of a snake between your teeth – the boy takes the head and the girl takes the tail.

b) You simply join hands and swap rings.

c) The boy's cloak is tied to the girl's blouse.

10 There is a final feast with alcohol to drink. But only certain people are allowed to drink. Who can booze?

a) You and your friends.

b) Everyone except the bride and groom.

c) Any guests over the age of 30.

Answers: All **c)** answers are correct. All **a)** and **b)** answers are wrong.

1 Boys, choose your bride. It has to be someone of your own position in society. You must use an old woman as the messenger to carry your proposal. Your granny would do.

2 Ask the girl's family if you can marry her. Don't bother asking the girl herself because you don't need her permission.

3 Send your messenger to ask your teacher if you can marry! If the teacher says 'No!' then you won't be allowed.

HOW COME EVERYONE ELSE AROUND HERE HAS A CHANCE TO OBJECT EXCEPT ME?

4 Choose the wedding day. This needs to be a 'good' day on the Aztec calendar. Perhaps you could look up your horoscope in a book? Saturdays are good days.

5 The girl's family organizes a feast at her house which guests eat while she has her wedding dress and make-up put on.

6 After dinner you must wait until dark because marriages take place at night. The bride is carried on the back of an old woman to the boy's house. If your granny isn't worn out with all the running around maybe she can carry the bride.

7 Guests follow in a procession by the light of torches – flaming torches, not electric torches, of course.

8 The couple sit on a mat spread in front of the fire and everyone gives them wedding presents. (Note: the Aztecs didn't have pop-up toasters, stainless steel butter dishes or electric kettles so don't give them.)

9 The couple are married when the boy's cloak is tied to the girl's blouse. This is still known today as tying the knot.

10 There's another feast (if you've recovered from the one at the girl's house!). This time the guests over the age of 30 can drink alcohol and it is no disgrace to get drunk. (Warning: Anyone under 30 getting drunk faces a beating for this crime. The next time they are caught they will be executed!)

How did you score?
10 Cheat
5 - 9 Lucky
1 - 4 Get your brain cells cleaned
0 You would make a really good Aztec sacrifice

Now, boys, if you enjoyed that why not try it again with another girl . . . and again with another girl . . . and again with another girl. And again and again and again. How many wives can you afford?

King Nezahualpilli had 2,000 wives and 144 children. How on earth did he remember their names? And, talking about kings . . .

The new emperor's new clothes

In Britain the monarchs have been crowned for over a thousand years in the richest robes money can buy. Thick silks, warm velvets and fur-trimmed collars. Very cosy in London fogs and Edinburgh drizzle.

The kings and queens dressed up as if to say, 'Look how grand I am, you peasants!'

But a new Aztec emperor did the opposite. He was taken in front of the sun god and had to tell the god what a feeble little human being he really was.

The emperor spent four days fasting (or three days if he was really, really fast!).

Then he took off all his clothes and stood in front of the statue of the god and said . . .

Oh master, oh night, oh wind, I am so poor. How can I work for this city? How can I work for its people? For I am blind, I am deaf, I am brainless and I am covered in filth. Maybe you've made a mistake and you are looking for someone else to rule?

Imagine the shock he'd get if the god said, 'All right, mate, get your kit on and push off. I'll find someone better!'

Of course all this 'humble' business didn't last long . . . it never does with emperors and kings. As soon as the coronation was over he went off to a feast where . . .

- every great lordly guest had to wear plain, simple clothes so they didn't look more grand than the emperor
- they had to bow their heads
- they were not allowed to look at the emperor's face
- they were not allowed to turn their back on him so they had to walk out of his room backwards.

84

From then on . . .

- he was carried almost everywhere in a chair shaded by a canopy of precious feathers
- if he did decide to step down then nobles swept the ground in front of him and covered the ground with cloths so his feet never touched the earth
- whenever he ate he was shielded from the ordinary people by a screen of gold
- he was offered a choice of a hundred dishes of food at each meal
- he was entertained by clowns and jugglers while he ate
- he had a palace aviary with ten rooms full of birds and a palace zoo filled with animals from all over his empire – rattlesnakes were kept on a bed of feathers.

What a humble sort of life! And all he had to do was take his clothes off and admit to a stone statue he was stupid. Even you could do that!

Furious fighters

Aztec men lived to fight. When the war drum sounded every Aztec man was expected to pick up his weapons and join his group of about 800 men.

What other fantastic facts do you know about the Aztec warriors? Try this quirky quiz that Quetzalcoatl would quite quickly quomplete. Just answer True or False to the following . . .

1 Aztec warriors wore armour.

2 The Aztecs had wooden clubs, edged with stone blades that were powerful enough to cut off a horse's head.

3 Aztec leaders were easy to spot because they wore large feather and reed constructions on their shoulders.

4 Aztec warriors believed that dying in battle was a wonderful thing.

5 Rich Aztec warriors wore gold and jewels when they went into battle.

6 Warriors didn't get their hair cut till they'd killed someone in battle.

7 Aztecs believed in killing themselves rather than being captured.

8 The Aztec army needed to capture 20 enemy fighters for sacrifice and no less.

9 Young Aztec men could be made full warriors by having their faces smeared with the blood of a heart that was still beating.

10 Warriors short of food would eat their dead friends.

Answers:

1 True. But it wasn't metal armour because they didn't have steel. It was a padded cotton coat, soaked in salt water to make it hard.

2 True. At least that's what the Spanish soldiers said when they fought against them. Before the Spanish arrived the Aztecs did NOT cut off horses, heads because there were no horses in Mexico.

3 True. This was fine when they were fighting other Mexican armies. But the Spanish invaders had guns and were able to pick out the leaders easily and then pick them off.

4 True. They believed that they were immediately turned into hummingbirds and hummed off to join the sun god in his heaven. Hummmm! A likely story.

5 True. Not just because they wanted to look cute as a corpse. They believed that precious stones had magical powers to protect them.

WELL, THEY'LL PROTECT HIS EARS ANYWAY

6 True. Young men had to leave some of their hair long – a disgraceful thing which told everyone that they weren't a real man yet.

7 False. King Moquiuhix tried to rebel against his Aztec friends. When his armies were defeated he threw himself off the top of his pyramid and died. The Aztec winners were so disgusted the dead king's body was not buried but left to rot.

8 True . . . but they sometimes took more. The Aztec Emperor Tizoc (ruled 1481 – 1486) ordered that every man in three defeated tribes should be executed. Not 20 – but 20,000.

9 True. Even the Tlaxcallan friends of the Spanish performed this ritual while the Christian Spanish soldiers looked on.

10 False. Warriors were happy to eat dead enemies but refused to eat the friends they had fought with, no matter how hungry they were. In the 1521 battle against the Spanish they boiled the bark of trees and ate that but left thousands of their dead friends untouched.

The gory games

The Maya played a ball game that was later copied by the Aztecs.

The Maya called it pok-a-tok, which sounds quite jolly – rather like ping-pong. The idea was that the better you played the 'ball game', the happier the gods would be and the better the crops would grow.

The ball game was linked with the ideas of human sacrifice and death. If you want to live like an Aztec then you may like to try this with a few friends. If you simply want to live . . . then don't ever play it!

You need:

- A court 140 metres long and 36 metres wide in the shape of an 'I'. The court is surrounded by stone walls. If that's a bit too big then try a basketball or netball court.
- A ring at each side of the court about 5 metres above the ground.
- Flat stones, carved in the shape of heads, to show the score.
- A rubber ball about 15 cm across.
- Two teams of about 10 a side – allow plenty of substitutes for players killed or carried off to hospital during the game.
- A 'skull rack' to hold the heads of sacrifice victims who'll be watching the game.
- Each player needs a helmet, and arm, knee and leg protectors made from boiled leather. (But don't go killing cows or cutting up shoes for their leather – skateboard protectors will do . . . or simply don't play as rough as the Aztecs!)

The aim:

As in basketball the players of a team pass the ball among themselves till they are in a position to score. A score is made by putting the ball through one of the rings set in the wall.

The rules:

You can use arms and legs to pass the ball but you must not use hands or feet . . . and that's about it really! That's probably why players were often killed during a game — there were no rules to stop you killing an opponent, and losing often meant disgrace, which made killing the opposition a very good idea. So you might want to add a rule that makes killing an opponent a foul.

The result:

The team that scores first is the winner. Some historians say losing players were taken to a platform at the side of the pitch where their heads were cut off and stuck on wooden poles. (Although you might find that a smack in the loser's face with a stale kipper may be enough of a winning celebration.) A player who scored through the hoop could claim any jewellery or clothing from the spectators. The problem was the player would have to catch the spectator first.

Sometimes the teams can agree on prizes that the winner gets. You could gamble with gold, jade, slaves or even a house . . . but ask your parents before you bet your house on the result.

The truth about the ball game
Historians don't always know the truth about ancient worlds. They guess.

Most history books will tell you that the Mayan and Aztec 'ball game' was played to the death. But other historians say that is quite silly.

The truth is there were pictures carved into the walls of the ball courts. These pictures showed a ball game in which the losers lost their heads. But the pictures didn't tell the tale of a real ball game – all they did was tell the tale of a ball game that happened in an ancient legend.

So that's the story told on the walls of the ball courts. A story made up to explain why the planet Venus disappears from our skies then comes back again.

When tourists arrived in the Mayan ball courts their guides said, 'This is what happened when they played the ball game – the losers lost their heads.'

Then historians took this story and repeated it in their books. (Check your own school books on the Maya and Aztecs.) It is probably not true!

History can be horrible . . . but historians can sometimes be horribler.

A game you wouldn't want to try . . .
Volador
You need:
- A pole – tall and solid like a Maypole with a platform on top.
- Four ropes attached to the top.
- Bird costumes.

The rules:
Four players dress up as birds, climb to the top of the pole and fasten the ropes under their arms. Each bird jumps off the top of the pole and swings round it 13 times. When four players have swung round 13 times they have created the lucky number 52 and this will make sure the Sun god continues to fly around the earth.

The result:
Nothing really. Just a sort of Aztec team-bungee-jump in honour of the Sun god, and a lot less messy than heart sacrifices.

94

Foul for females

Women were not very well treated in the Aztec world. But they could do one thing that would make men respect them . . . they could die giving birth. That was the bravest thing a woman could do, the men said.

The unfortunate woman's ghost haunted crossroads at night. It was very unlucky to meet her. But Aztecs didn't think the dead woman's body was unlucky. Quite the opposite, they believed it had magical powers. If an Aztec warrior could just cut off a finger and some hair from her body then he could fasten it on to his shield when he went to war. The magic finger would protect him.

How did he get his hands on the fingers? Did he go to the dead woman's family and say, 'Excuse me, would you mind if I cut up her body?'

No. They were Aztecs and Aztecs never do anything so polite or simple.

When warriors heard about a suitable corpse they would get together in a gang and ambush the funeral. (Of course there couldn't be more than ten in the gang – that would make sure that everyone got a finger!)

If they missed the funeral then it still wasn't too late. They could find the grave and dig up the body!

One minute it's 'rest in peace' and the next minute it's 'rest in pieces'!

And, talking about graveyards . . .

Magical medicine and murderous mines

The emperor lived in his palace with some rooms large enough for 3,000 visitors. Aztec villagers lived in huts built from sun-dried bricks and whitewashed. They would have three or four rooms and enough space for 10 to 15 people to live . . . and die.

Because . . . when a member of the family died then they were buried under the floor of the house! This was another idea copied from the Maya. Imagine guzzling your grub over granny or sleeping over sister or drinking over Dad! Yeuch!

NOTE: This is NOT a very healthy thing to do, so don't bury your favourite goldfish under the floorboards.

If you do fall ill, then do NOT try Aztec cures. The useless ones don't work and the working ones could kill the patient. Some are still used today because the herbs worked and some seem just plain silly to us. Still, there's no harm in trying . . .

Curing an Aztec cold

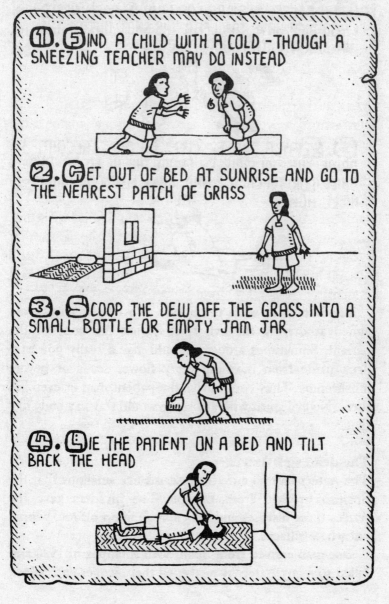

1. FIND A CHILD WITH A COLD — THOUGH A SNEEZING TEACHER MAY DO INSTEAD

2. GET OUT OF BED AT SUNRISE AND GO TO THE NEAREST PATCH OF GRASS

3. SCOOP THE DEW OFF THE GRASS INTO A SMALL BOTTLE OR EMPTY JAM JAR

4. LIE THE PATIENT ON A BED AND TILT BACK THE HEAD

5. PLACE ONE DROP OF DEW IN EACH NOSTRIL. (YOU MAY HAVE TO CLEAR THE SNOT OUT OF THE WAY FIRST WITH A GOOD BLOW)

6. SAY A PRAYER LIKE 'OH QUETZALCOATL, DRIVE THE EVIL SPIRITS FROM THE HEAD OF THIS CHILD (OR TEACHER) AND MAKE HER (OR HIM) WELL AGAIN'

The important bit is the prayer. Most Aztec cures were aimed at driving the evil spirits from the body of the patient. Sometimes a doctor would give a really powerful drug made from morning glory flower seeds or peyote mushrooms. They could drive the patient mad or even kill them. No evil spirit with any sense would stay in a body like that!

The dead sick Aztecs

The Aztecs had no cure for diseases like smallpox that the Spanish brought from Europe. The invaders gave the Aztecs these diseases and they spread like a plague, wiping out whole villages.

One man arrived from Spain with smallpox in 1520 and killed so many Aztecs it weakened their armies and helped the Spanish to win.

Other diseases, like measles, whooping cough, yellow fever and malaria wiped out millions more. It was worse than the Black Death in Europe! If the diseases didn't get them then the exhausting work in the silver mines and the field did.

It's a mystery where the Maya went.

Where did the Aztecs go? No mystery. This is where they went . . .

Of course all of this ripping out of living hearts made the Aztecs very unpopular with the tribes that they ruled. The only hope for the suffering Mexicans lay in an ancient legend.

In this legend the Mexican people had come from another land and their leader was a god called Quetzalcoatl. This great hero had been driven from Mexico on a raft of snakes but he said he'd return one day.

The legend said that in the First Year of the Reed Quetzalcoatl would arrive with a sword and the Mexicans would recognize him because he would be a bearded white man. Quetzalcoatl would end the reign of the Aztec bullies and bring peace to Mexico.

Well, when Hernan Cortés and the Spanish landed, the legend got most of it right!

Hernan Cortés and his 600 soldiers began their conquest. With the use of guns – and with a lot of luck – they battled their way through the Aztec empire.

Crafty Cortés

Hernan Cortés set off for Mexico with 11 ships, 508 soldiers and about a hundred sailors. He also had 16 horses. The horses were going to be very important to him in battles. The people of Mexico had never seen horses before.

Cortés didn't know that the Aztecs ruled over 20 million people, but he guessed he couldn't hope to conquer the whole empire with his little army. He had to use his brains. He had to win the friendship of the natives and he had to impress them with his force.

Are you as crafty as Cortés? What would you have done in these tricky situations?

The problem of the looter

Cortés had a strict rule that said his men must not steal from the defeated tribes. That was called 'looting' and was punished by death.

Shortly after Cortés had landed he began to make friends with some of the Mexican tribes who hated the Aztecs. As they marched forward some of his Mexican friends, the Zempoalans, began looting Cingapacinga villages. Cortés was angry and explained the rule against looting. 'Give back all you have taken,' he ordered.

The Zempoalans did as they were told. Cortés now had more friends – the Cingapacinga liked him too!

But then a very embarrassing thing happened. One of Cortés's own Spanish soldiers was caught looting. What could Cortés do? He was given differing advice . . .

(A) YOU HAVE TO HANG THE MAN. YOU MUST SHOW THE MEXICANS THAT YOUR LAWS ARE FAIR AND THE SAME FOR EVERYONE. THE MEXICANS MAY DESERT YOU IF YOU DON'T HANG HIM.

(B) YOU CANNOT HANG THE MAN. YOU NEED EVERY SPANISH SOLDIER YOU HAVE ALIVE. YOUR OWN SOLDIERS MAY DESERT YOU IF YOU HANG HIM.

They were both right! It looked as though Cortés would lose the support of his 500 conquistadors or the support of 2,000 Zempoalan warriors.

Would you follow Advice A or Advice B? Or would you accept the advice of both and lose no support at all? How could Cortés possibly do that?

TIE A ROPE AROUND THE MAN'S NECK AND HOIST HIM UP ON THAT TREE. WE WILL MARCH OFF. AS SOON AS WE ARE OUT OF SIGHT CUT THE FOOL DOWN BEFORE HE STRANGLES TO DEATH.

THAT'S CRAFTY CORTÉS

Cortés still had problems with some of his soldiers who wanted to steal a ship and sail back home. How did he solve that problem?

He burned all the ships, of course. Crafty Cortés!

The power of the priests

Cortés wanted to stop the human sacrifices – about five a day in the 'friendly' towns he was marching through. He wanted to convert the Mexicans to Christianity. The problem was that the Mexican priests were awesome men.

A Spanish writer said . . .

They wore black cloaks and their hair down to their waists. Some even wore their hair down to their feet, and

> *it was so clotted and matted with blood that it could not be pulled apart. Their ears were cut to pieces as a sacrifice and they smelled of rotting flesh.*

These priests didn't want to give up their powerful positions. Cortés needed their support. What could he do?

> (A) EXECUTE THEM IF THEY WON'T GIVE UP THEIR POWER. OUR CHRISTIAN CHURCH WON'T SUPPORT THEIR BLOODTHIRSTY WAYS

> (B) IF YOU KILL THE PRIESTS THE MEXICANS WILL NOT LISTEN TO ANYONE ELSE

Would you follow Advice A or Advice B? Or could Cortés keep both the Church and the Mexicans happy?

> YOU CAN STAY IN POWER BY BECOMING CHRISTIAN PRIESTS! HAVE YOUR HAIR WASHED AND CUT. HAVE A BATH AND WEAR WHITE ROBES AND WE'LL SHOW YOU HOW TO HAVE CHRISTIAN SERVICES!

And it worked. The Aztec idols were thrown off the top of the pyramid and replaced with a Christian altar and cross. The bloodstains were covered with whitewash and the pyramid priests became Christian priests – at least that's what some people say.

The Christians came along and said to the Aztec priests, 'Eat this bread, it is the body of our Lord and drink this wine, it is his blood!' The priests could understand this! Eating humans gave you the powers of the dead human – eating bread and wine at a Christian 'communion' would give you the powers of a god! No wonder they agreed.

Cortés left the friendly towns with their converted priests and marched on to Tenochtitlan and the mighty Aztec Emperor, Motecuhzoma.

Sad superstitions

The Spanish were the winners and the Spanish wrote the history books. Like most 'winners' in history they changed the story and made up the facts to make themselves look right and the enemy look wrong.

The Spanish histories made Emperor Motecuhzoma look like a weak and stupid man who threw away his empire because he believed in silly superstitions and 'signs'.

But what were these strange signs … and what would you have thought if you'd seen them or heard about them?

Motecuhzoma sent for his magicians and asked them to explain these terrifying signs. If you had been one of the magicians, how would you have explained them?

If you were a clever magician you'd have said . . .

Well? Would you have come up with the right answers? If you didn't . . . and Motecuhzoma's magicians didn't . . . then you would have suffered like them. A slow death by cruel torture.

The bad news is that there were some things that even a modern smart-Alec like you couldn't explain. Motecuhzoma also claimed to have experienced the following . . .

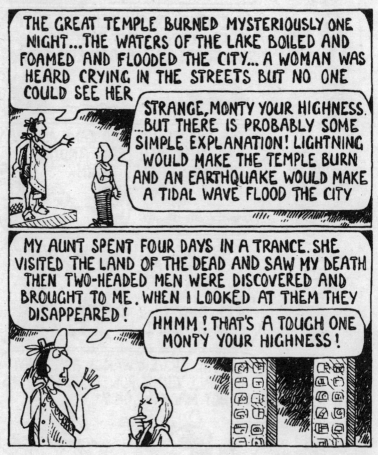

THE GREAT TEMPLE BURNED MYSTERIOUSLY ONE NIGHT...THE WATERS OF THE LAKE BOILED AND FOAMED AND FLOODED THE CITY... A WOMAN WAS HEARD CRYING IN THE STREETS BUT NO ONE COULD SEE HER

STRANGE, MONTY YOUR HIGHNESS ...BUT THERE IS PROBABLY SOME SIMPLE EXPLANATION! LIGHTNING WOULD MAKE THE TEMPLE BURN AND AN EARTHQUAKE WOULD MAKE A TIDAL WAVE FLOOD THE CITY

MY AUNT SPENT FOUR DAYS IN A TRANCE. SHE VISITED THE LAND OF THE DEAD AND SAW MY DEATH THEN TWO-HEADED MEN WERE DISCOVERED AND BROUGHT TO ME. WHEN I LOOKED AT THEM THEY DISAPPEARED!

HMMM! THAT'S A TOUGH ONE MONTY YOUR HIGHNESS!

AND, WORST OF ALL, VILLAGERS BROUGHT A BIRD TO ME. WHEN I LOOKED AT ITS FOREHEAD THERE WAS A MIRROR. AND IN THE MIRROR I SAW STARS THOUGH IT WAS DAYLIGHT! AND THE NEXT TIME I LOOKED I SAW ARMED MEN ON THE BACKS OF DEER! EXPLAIN THAT... OR DIE!

ERRRR! THERE IS REALLY ONLY ONE EXPLANATION, MONTY YOUR HIGHNESS! YOU'RE A FEW BRICKS SHORT OF A PYRAMID!

Motecuhzoma's problem was that he didn't have enough friends to help him! The people of Tlaxcallan hated the Aztecs – not surprising since the Aztecs had spent 100 years trying to enslave them and sacrifice them. The Tlaxcallan people joined the Spanish and made Cortés's little band into an army of 5,000 warriors.

The truth is Motecuhzoma probably didn't believe Hernan Cortés was the god Quetzalcoatl on earth. The reason Motecuhzoma welcomed Cortés was that he believed he was a messenger from another great king . . . which he was! Naturally he welcomed this messenger as an important visitor. Imagine the shock when the visitor entered the royal palace . . . and made emperor Motecuhzoma a prisoner!

The city of horrors
Motecuhzoma had messages that Cortés and his small army had landed on the coast. The emperor tried everything to

keep Cortés and the conquistadors out of Tenochtitlan, the capital city. He'd tried to bribe Cortés with gold, frighten him off with threats and kill him off with an ambush that failed.

In the end he just sat back and waited for the conquistadors to arrive.

On 8 November 1519 the Spaniard marched across the causeway to the island city of Tenochtitlan and came face-to-face with the Aztec emperor.

Cortés himself wrote down Motecuhzoma's welcoming speech . . .

> *We have known for a long time that neither I nor the people who live here are the original inhabitants. We know it belongs to strangers who come from distant parts. We always knew that they would return one day to rule us. We will obey you and all that we own is yours.*

THAT'S JOLLY NICE OF YOU

Great news! The emperor himself was handing over power. The Spanish moved into the great palace of Motecuhzoma's father – and it was large enough to hold them all.

It gave the Spaniards a wonderful view, but they weren't too keen on what they saw. They looked out on the Great Pyramid for a start. A Spaniard called Tapia wrote . . .

> *At the top was a room with the greatest god of all the land. It was three metres high. He was made from seeds that were ground up into flour then mixed into a paste with the blood of boys and girls.*
>
> *There were more than 5,000 people in the service of this god. They rose promptly at midnight for their sacrifice which was letting blood from the tongue, the arms and the thighs, wetting straws with the blood and offering them to a huge oak-wood fire.*

Spaniard Bernal Diaz was most shocked by the 'skull rack' near the main gate to the temple. It was like a hat rack . . . but for skulls. Hundreds of skulls were set in cement into a sloping wall and seventy tall poles stood on top, each pole with dozens of pegs. Diaz went on . . .

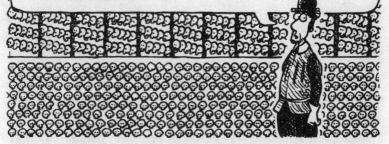

> *Each peg had five skulls on. A total of 136,000 skulls were counted and this did not include the countless skulls that made up the walls.*

Still, the Spaniards managed to create their own horrors in that nightmare city. A rebel chief and his sons were brought to the city for execution. Cortés ordered that they should be burned alive at the stake.

The Mexicans were used to seeing heart sacrifices by the thousand. But the whole city turned out to watch this new type of execution. They watched in silence.

Cortés had done something even Motecuhzoma hadn't managed in the city of horrors. He had shocked the Aztecs.

The angry Aztecs
Burning Mexican chiefs did not stir the Aztecs to fight against Cortés and the little Spanish force. But the Spanish made two mistakes which made the Aztecs finally rebel.

First, Cortés went into their sacrifice temple in the capital Tenochtitlan. An Indian historian described what Cortés did next . . .

> *Cortés ordered the priests to bring water to wash the blood off the walls and he told them to take the statues of their gods away. The priests laughed and said they could not move their gods. So Cortés replied, 'It will give me great pleasure to fight for my god against your gods who are nothing.' He took up an iron bar and began to smash their statues.*

The priests were horrified and the Aztec people in the city were furious. The angry Aztecs may have planned to kill the Spaniards after that. They asked the conquistadors if they could hold their great harvest festival dance at the temple and invited the soldiers to watch.

The soldiers heard a rumour that the Aztecs planned to kill them straight after the dance . . . so the soldiers struck first. An Indian wrote . . .

They ran in among the dancers and attacked the man who was drumming and cut off his arms. They cut off his head and it rolled across the floor. Then they attacked the dancers, stabbing them, spearing them and striking some with their swords. They attacked some from behind and these fell instantly to the ground with their entrails hanging out. Some attempted to run away but their intestines dragged as they ran; they seemed to tangle their feet in their own entrails. Others they beheaded; they cut off their heads or split their heads to pieces. No matter how they tried to save themselves, they could find no escape.

Now the Aztecs organized themselves and attacked the Spaniards with huge forces. The Aztec Emperor, Motecuhzoma, tried telling his people that the Spanish were their friends. The people threw rocks and fired arrows at Motecuhzoma. A rock hit the emperor on the head and he died three days later.[1]

1. Enemies of Cortés accused him of murdering Motecuhzoma since he was no more use to him. That's probably not true. The people who wrote that weren't there at the time.

Finally the ferocious Aztecs drove the Spanish out of their capital Tenochtitlan and killed two-thirds of them – many of the Spanish drowned when they slipped into the lake because of the stolen gold they had strapped to their bodies.

The Spanish conquest of Mexico was finished after just eight months . . . at least, it was finished for the moment.

Quick quiz

One of Cortés's captains, Pedro Alvarado, was fighting his way across the bridge over the lake. He was on horseback and armed with a lance. His horse was killed so he battled on with just his lance. At last he reached a place where the bridge had been broken. It was just too far for a man in armour to jump across. What would you have done . . . and what did Alvarado do?

Answer: He pole-vaulted across using his lance! This spot is now part of the roadway out of Mexico City and it's still called Alvarado's Leap.

Battling back

But Hernan Cortés wasn't going to give up the treasures of the Aztecs that easily. In 1521 he returned.

This was an important day in the Aztec world . . . and the

Spanish world too. It would have made headline news if they'd had headlines. Or even if they'd had newspapers. You can just picture it . . .

el BINGO!

13 August 1521

el SoL

≈ PRICE ≈
Still only two pieces of eight!
(or sixteen pieces of one)

EXCLUSIVE:

HAPPY HERNAN GOES FOR GOLD

Just two years after landing on the filthy-rich Aztec shores, cool Conquistador Cortés (36) has captured their capital! Today his brave little army marched into the Aztec city of Tenochtitlan and he has emperor Cuahtemoc under arrest. The battle for Tenochtitlan raged non-stop for 93 days.

The battle was fierce and the wounded Cortés was being dragged to captivity by an Aztec chief. The chief stopped dragging him when Captain Olea hacked off the Aztec's arm! It was a big Aztec mistake. They had tried to take Cortés alive so they could sacrifice him. If they'd killed him when they had the chance then the Spaniards could have lost the whole war.

A tired but happy Cortés told our reporter, 'My men did well. When we landed here we had no idea the place was so big. Otherwise

115

we might have given up before we even started!'

The Spanish fought bravely because they saw what happened to their comrades who were captured. They watched in horror as Spanish prisoners were dragged to the top of the temple pyramid, had their beating hearts ripped out and their bodies kicked down the steps to butchers waiting below.

Footsore soldiers agreed. 'We were all for going home as soon as we got here,' Private Christofer Robino (24) agreed. 'But Captain-General Cortés burned our boats so we had to go forward. Unless we wanted to sail back to Spain on a lump of charcoal!' he laughed.

Hoards of Aztec treasure are awaiting the clever conquerors but first they have to clean up the city. Our reporter says it is an amazing place, built on an island and surrounded by farms on artificial islands. There are about 200,000 people living in the city and as many as 60,000 come to the Tenochtitlan market from all over the empire. The peasants live in wood and mud houses but the nobles and priests live in fine stone palaces.

But the real horror hovers in the centre. The city centre is dominated by the temples – huge stepped pyramids, plastered with brilliant colours. But the colours are stained by crusted dried blood and the stench of death in the midday sun has turned the stomachs of the strongest soldiers.

Captain-General Cortés has big plans for terrible Tenochtitlan and its awful

Aztec cannibals. He is planning to convert the natives to Christianity then he'll flatten the evil city to the ground. 'If the Indians don't convert to Christianity then we'll torture them and execute them until they do,' he said grimly. 'That'll put a stop to all this cruel killing.'

Hernan Cortés was made Governor of the country, which was renamed New Spain. The Aztecs had been rubbed out of history; the Spaniards destroyed their great capital of Tenochtitlan utterly, the Spanish priests destroyed the Aztec statues, their libraries and their picture-writings.

Cortés then sent one of his generals, Francisco de Montejo, to conquer the tribes who remained in the old Mayan kingdom. By 1546 the northern Mayan cities had been defeated with dreadful slaughter and half a million Maya were sold into slavery. The Itza tribe hid in the dense jungles and stayed free until 1697. Then the Spanish arrived and crushed this last tribe of old Mexico.

Of course the killing didn't stop when Cortés defeated the Aztecs. The Aztec peasants became slaves and were worked to death by the Spanish conquerors. Spanish settlers took over the Aztec lands – the Spanish priests converted the Aztecs to Christianity: the great blood-stained pyramids were pulled down and the rubble from them used to build a Christian cathedral. The sacrifices stopped . . . but people carried on being killed.

Conquistadors conquered

You may be pleased to hear that the Spanish conquistadors didn't have it all their own way. Stealing the treasure of the

Aztecs was easy compared to their next task . . . getting it back across the Atlantic to their king in Spain.

Three fat, slow transport ships set off from Mexico in 1523. Conquistador Cortés wrote:

> *I am sending you things so marvellous that they cannot be described in writing, nor can they be understood without seeing them*

These 'marvellous things' included jaguar and puma cats, sugar, emeralds, topazes, carved masks encrusted with jewels, feathered cloaks of Aztec priests, red-yellow-blue macaws, talking parrots, Aztec slaves, rings, shields, helmets, vases and polished stone mirrors. The pearls alone weighed 300 kg and there was 220 kg of gold dust, three huge cases of gold ingots and other cases of silver bars.

The gold and silver never made it to Spain . . . and neither did some of the Spanish conquistadors as extracts from the ship's log show . . .

| Day 17 | Sickness has killed eleven of our crew in the first two weeks. Weather bad, ship leaking and progress slow. |
| Day 24 | Storm smashed wooden cage last night. Jaguar escaped. Beast tore arm off one sailor, ripped leg off soldier and clawed open shoulder of third before it leapt overboard. Two men died. Officers elect to |

Day 87 Reached Azores. Commander Quixones went ashore with officers but returned quarrelling about a woman they had met. Officer split Quixones, skull with his cutlass. Commander Quixones, body thrown overboard for sharks and brains washed off deck with sea-water.

Day 133 French pirates have damaged two of our ships and boarded them. Only this ship will ever reach Spain. We tried to fight but our powder is defective after months at sea. King Carlos will not be pleased.

King Carlos was furious. But for the next 200 years the Spanish would have to get used to being robbed by pirates waiting, like vultures, to tear the riches from the treasure ships.

The Quetzalcoatl quiz

Now that you know everything your teacher never knew about the Aztecs, you can torture Sir or Miss even more. No, not by ripping out their heart with a stone-age knife. By testing their brain cell with these fiendishly foul questions. (If you can't torment a teacher then pester a parent – and if your parents run screaming you'll just have to test yourself!)

1 What sort of knife did the priests use to cut out a victim's heart?
a) glass
b) bronze
c) gold

2 The name Quetzalcoatl means what?
a) white man with beard
b) a coat decorated with quartz stones
c) a snake with feathers

3 Before the Aztecs came the Toltecs and before the Toltecs came the Olmecs. The Olmecs were known as what?
a) the green monkey people
b) the rubber people
c) the cactus-haired people

4 Aztec children were given the job of collecting things in the fields. What did they collect?
a) berries
b) beetles
c) bat droppings

URGH LOOK! BAT DROPPINGS WITH BEETLE-BERRIES IN THEM

5 Aztecs were told what to wear. Poor people wore simple clothing and lords wore rich clothing. What was the punishment for a poor person caught wearing rich clothes for a second time?

a) death

b) being stripped

c) having their house knocked down

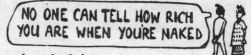

6 The Aztecs asked the Spanish conquerors if they could go to their temple for a harvest festival dance. The Spanish agreed. What happened when the Aztecs arrived?

a) They were preached to by Christian priests.

b) They were told that sacrifices in the temple were banned from now on.

c) They were massacred.

7 The Aztec traders became very rich and dressed in fine clothes. But the emperor would have hated this. So what did they do?

a) They had to wear a plain white cloth over the top of their fine clothes. It reached down to their ankles.

b) They wore a reversible coat. It was rich on the outside but they could turn it round quickly if the emperor appeared to show a plain side.

c) They had to creep into the city at night so no one, especially the emperor, could see them.

8 When the Spanish arrived in Mexico they noticed little wooden huts on the side of the road in both the country and the town. Aztecs popped in for a couple of minutes before coming out again looking content. What were the little wooden huts?

a) public toilets

b) Aztec national lottery shops

c) Aztec pubs for drinking maize wine

9 How did Aztecs keep their teeth clean?

a) They had toothpicks made from cactus spines.

b) They used chewing gum.

c) They made toothpaste from powdered stone in cream.

10 The Spanish discovered the Aztecs had lots of gold and they tricked them out of it by saying, 'We need your gold . . . '

a) '. . . to give to the poor and the hungry natives.'

b) '. . . to make you metal guns like ours which we'll give you for hunting.'

c) '. . . because it's the only thing that will cure you of your disease.'

Answers:

1a) The knives were made of a type of natural glass that came from hardened volcanic lava. It is called 'obsidian' and can be polished to look really sharp, shiny and attractive. It's used to make jewellery now.

2c) Quetzalcoatl was a serpent or snake with plumes or feathers. How could the Aztecs mistake a Spanish soldier for a snake with feathers? They must be a bit short-sighted. No wonder the Spanish beat them so easily!

3b) The Olmecs were NOT called the rubber people because they were like bendy toys. They got their name because they lived in the area where rubber trees grew – until the Toltecs rubbed them out, of course. No one knows what name the Olmecs called themselves.

4b) The Aztec children collected female scale beetles that live on cactus plants. These beetles were crushed and used to make red dye for clothes, called cochineal.

The Spanish invaders brought the idea back to Europe and it is still used in places as food dye. The Aztecs needed 150,000 beetles to make one kilo of dye. The Aztecs dyed – the beetles simply died.

5a) A peasant trying to pose as a posh person had their house knocked down the first time they were caught. If they tried it again they would be executed. And you thought school uniforms were a rotten idea?

6c) The Spanish killed them. And, as we've seen, this made the surviving Aztecs angrier and fight even harder to throw out the Spanish bullies.

7c) The merchants had to creep around after dark when they returned from trading. There was another way to keep them fairly poor and a little more humble. The richer they were the greater the feasts they had to give to the nobles. They were forced to give rich presents to their guests . . . and buy fine slaves in the market to be sacrificed. Imagine having a birthday party where you give all the presents!

8a) The Aztecs needed human 'manure' to spread on their fields so they encouraged people to use public toilets. The toilets would be emptied on to the soil to make it richer and help the pumpkins and maize grow better. But don't worry – your cornflakes won't have been grown with human manure . . . probably just lots of chemicals, weed-killers and pest-killers. Haven't things improved since Aztec times?

9b) Aztecs chewed chicle gum made from a milky fluid inside some trees and plants. It is still used for chewing gum today. Some things never change. The Aztecs didn't like people who chewed in public and especially those who made popping and snapping noises with the gum . . . just like some children do in their classrooms! And today's teachers don't like that either. Something else that hasn't changed!

10c) The sad Aztecs believed that the Spanish conquerors would use the gold to cure them of the diseases that had come from Europe. What was this disease supposed to be? Gold fever?

EPILOGUE

Some historians try to make excuses for the Aztecs. They say, 'The Aztecs lived in violent times and had to be ruthless and bloodthirsty to survive.'

That may have been true at the start of their rise to power. But they began to enjoy the cruelty. That is harder for us to forgive . . . and it led to their downfall in the end.

When Emperor Tizoc wanted a sacrifice he believed that he needed 20 warriors to die on the pyramid in Tenochtitlan. Instead he decided to terrify all the other tribes in Mexico with a huge massacre. He took every single man from three Mixtec tribes, 20,000 men, and sent them for sacrifice.

The victims had eagle feathers stuck to them with their own blood and were led to the Aztec capital. They were all killed on the pyramid. The Aztecs killed the first ones then the priests took over. In early sacrifices the people had eaten small parts of the victims. This time there were too many. They were simply killed and their bodies thrown into the marshes.

It terrified the other tribes in Mexico all right. But it also disgusted them. They learned to hate the Aztecs. They knew they would have to wait, but one day their chance would come to overthrow the vicious, heart-ripping people.

And that chance came when the Spaniards arrived. If the Aztecs had been popular then all the people of Mexico would have joined together to drive them back to Spain. Instead they turned against the Aztecs and destroyed them. Sadly the Spaniards just said, 'Thanks very much!' and took over from the terrors of Tenochtitlan.

An Aztec poem moaned . . .

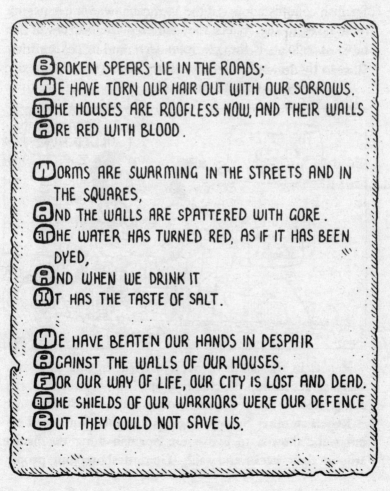

BROKEN SPEARS LIE IN THE ROADS;
WE HAVE TORN OUR HAIR OUT WITH OUR SORROWS.
THE HOUSES ARE ROOFLESS NOW, AND THEIR WALLS
ARE RED WITH BLOOD.

WORMS ARE SWARMING IN THE STREETS AND IN
    THE SQUARES,
AND THE WALLS ARE SPATTERED WITH GORE.
THE WATER HAS TURNED RED, AS IF IT HAS BEEN
    DYED,
AND WHEN WE DRINK IT
IT HAS THE TASTE OF SALT.

WE HAVE BEATEN OUR HANDS IN DESPAIR
AGAINST THE WALLS OF OUR HOUSES.
FOR OUR WAY OF LIFE, OUR CITY IS LOST AND DEAD.
THE SHIELDS OF OUR WARRIORS WERE OUR DEFENCE
BUT THEY COULD NOT SAVE US.

The hideously bloodstained pyramid in Tenochtitlan was blown up with 500 barrels of gunpowder. A Christian cathedral was built in its place. Things should have started to improve for the suffering Mexicans. But history is too horrible to allow 'happy ever after' endings.

Those Mexicans had slaved in the fields and died for the Aztecs. Now they slaved in the fields and died for the Spanish conquistadors – if the Mexicans were late in paying their taxes to the Aztecs they suffered the horrors of the heart sacrifice – if the Mexicans were late in paying their taxes to the Spanish then they were burned to death.

Either way they ended up dead.

Rebels in the south of Mexico tried digging pits with sharp stakes to stop the charging Spanish horsemen ... the conquistadors threw the rebels on to their own stakes.

Rebels in other Spanish regions had their hands cut off but were allowed to live – the Spanish hung the hands around their necks and said, 'Go and show your people what happens to rebels.' And the conquistadors called the Aztecs savage!

The Mexicans had a good way of looking at death. A poem in the old Aztec language of Nahuatl puts it best. It said . . .

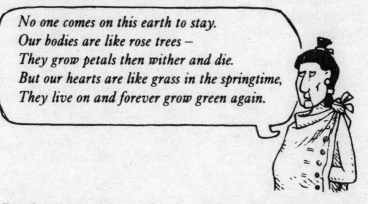

No one comes on this earth to stay.
Our bodies are like rose trees –
They grow petals then wither and die.
But our hearts are like grass in the springtime,
They live on and forever grow green again.

People come and go. So do nations. The Olmecs, the Toltecs, the Aztecs. All gone.

And, if you believe the ancient Mexican legends, the earth itself comes and goes. On 22 December 2012 it will be destroyed yet again.

Or will it? History can sometimes be horribly wrong!

We'll just have to wait and see.

2012?... WHERE THERE'S A WILL THERE'S A WAY

THE INCREDIBLE
INCAS

To Virginia Garrard-Burnett who proposed this book
and researched it. Sincere thanks.

INTRODUCTION

History can be horrible because history, like school, can be full of bullies ...

You'll be having a nice, peaceful life when along comes a bully and changes all that ...

Who do you feel sorry for? The victim, of course!

But history is never that simple. Sooner or later the bully will meet up with an even more scary bully – usually one with better weapons ...

Who do you feel sorry for now?

And what does the bully do when s/he's bullied? Give in and become a slave? Or stand up to the new bully?

The Incas were a bit like that. They came along and bullied the people of Peru into handing over their wealth. Then along came the Spanish invaders (the 'conquistadors') and turned the Incas into slaves.

So who do you feel sorry for?

To be honest there are no easy answers. That's why history is so horrible.

Of course school history books like questions with easy answers!

Question: 'When did the Spanish arrive in Peru?'

Answer: '1532.'

B-O-R-I-N-G!

But this is a horrible history and it will look at the questions that really matter. So trash that textbook and find out the terrible truth about the Incas ...

TIMELINE

Early Incan timeline

11,000 BC The first people settle in the area we now call Peru.

1250 BC Tribes of people begin to form in the Andes. They're called things like Chavin and Chimu, Nazca and Tiahuanaco.

AD 600 For a couple of hundred years the people from the Huari region will boss the western Andes. With them comes the spread of mummy burial. (That's corpses wrapped in cloth, not burying your mother.)

900 The Huari have gone (in a bit of a Huari) and the people split into tribes again. Most of these little states are no bigger than a single valley.

1105 Around this time the first Incan lord, Sinchi Roca, begins to rule his tribe, but his people are not very powerful … yet.

1370 The Chimu people are the biggest bullying bosses in Peru. They're led by Nancen Pinco who lives in Chan Chan. It seems as if these Chimu built a new palace for each new ruler and kept the old palaces going after the rulers died.

1438 The little Incan tribe starts to grow quickly and that means

135

trouble. Over the next fifty years the incredible Incas will conquer all the other tribes and rule them.

Incan Empire timeline

1100 The Incas start to spread out and conquer other people. Maybe a few years of dry weather left them low on food so they had to go out and pinch it.

1438 The Chanca people attack the Incas. They're defeated but the invasion starts the Incas fighting amongst themselves.

1492 Chris Columbus stumbles across America. He'll soon be followed by Spanish conquistadors who'll conquer the South American peoples. They haven't reached the Incan lands yet ... but give them time.

1525 A terrible plague sweeps through the Incan homeland – probably a disease like measles or smallpox brought from Europe. The Spanish aren't in Peru yet but their germs are!

Later we'll see what happens when the Spanish arrive ...

LEGENDARY LORDS

Where do humans come from? People have wondered this since they had two brain cells to think with.

Scientists say . . .

They could be right.

Christians say . . .

They could be right. The Bible reckons God made us in his image and some of us are very god-like, aren't we?

But the Incas came up with an even more sensible idea . . .

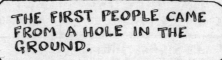

A bit like worms!

Lord number 1: Mighty Manco

There are three caves at Paqari-tampu where (they say) the first Incan leader first saw the light of day. His name was Manco Capac and he popped out of one of the caves with his three brothers and four sisters. Ten groups of people appeared from the other caves, but naturally the Incas were the leaders. Then they set off on a great journey through the Andes . . .

THEY LOOKED FOR GOOD SOIL TO FARM AND GROW CROPS. MANCO HAD A BRIGHT IDEA...

MY BROTHERS EAT TOO MUCH! THERE'LL BE MORE FOOD FOR THE REST OF US IF I KILL THEM!

THAT'S WHAT HE DID. ONE WAS SEALED IN A CAVE AND TWO WERE TURNED TO STONE. THEN HE DID SOMETHING VERY STRANGE...

I NEED A WIFE. I CAN'T MARRY ONE OF THE COMMON PEOPLE. I'LL MARRY MY SISTER, MAMA OCLLO!

HELP!

IN TIME THEY HAD CHILDREN...

LET'S CALL THIS LITTLE CHAP SINCHI ROCA

AT LAST THE INCAS ARRIVED AT CUZCO.

SEEMS LIKE A NICE PLACE!

Incan legends say Manco was the first of eight Lords of Cuzco – their valley in the Andes. No one is sure how true the stories about the eight lords are. The important thing is that most Incas *believed* these stories.

Lord number 2: Super Sinchi

Another story says that when Manco Capac died there were lots of his children who could have taken his place. The people all wanted Sinchi Roca . . . but Sinchi was NOT expected to take the throne ahead of his brothers.

How did he do it? With a bit of help from his mum! Would you like to be the next Prime Minister/President/King/Queen of your country? Here's how Mama Ocllo fixed it for Sinchi . . .

The trick seemed to work and Sinchi Roca was made the new Lord of Cuzco.

Stylish Sinchi

Sinchi was much more peaceful than dead old Manco. He spent less time murdering people and more time inventing things. What was his greatest invention? It was something that would show all the people who the royal family were, at a glance.

What did super Sinchi invent?

a) golden crowns   **b)** purple robes   **c)** fringe hairstyles

Answer: **c)** Yes, Sinchi Roca said that the Incan rulers would have their hair cut straight across the forehead.

Sinchi Roca started another new trend after he died! He was the first of the Incan lords to be turned into a mummy. The corpse was kept so well it was put on show in Cuzco two hundred years after he died.

Lord number 3: Lovely Lloque

Third emperor (Lloque Yupanqui) was a pretty peaceful bloke compared to Manco. Even though he didn't go around flattening farmers, looting lands and ruling ruthlessly he was still remembered as . . .

Surprisingly enough, Lloque was called 'left-handed' because . . . he was left-handed.

Unforgettable? Well anyone who looked at Lloque would never forget him. That face would haunt your dreams for ever. He was simply the *ugliest* man anyone had ever seen! His sad story is soon told . . .

- People who saw him ran away.
- His chief wife couldn't stand the sight of him.
- He had no children with his chief wife.
- He was advised to take the daughter of a neighbouring chief for a wife – she couldn't stand the sight of him either.
- Her father forced her to marry Lloque and she gave birth to Mayta Capac.

Unforgettably ugly – do you know anyone like that?

Lord number 4: Mighty Mayta Capac

The fourth Lord of Cuzco, Mayta Capac, was big trouble from the moment he was born.

- Legend said that he was born six months before he was due.
- As a newborn baby he was strong and had all his teeth.
- By the time he was a year old he was as big as an eight-year-old. (Imagine the size of his nappies!)

Mayta ruled in the 1300s and began invading the tribes next to Cuzco valley. What was it that made Mayta such a nasty neighbour? The weather!

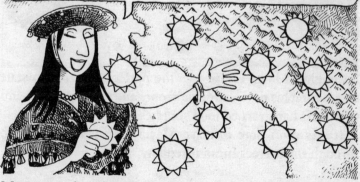

... AND DRY WEATHER IS FORECAST FOR THE NEXT FEW YEARS. CROPS WILL BE POOR, PEOPLE WILL STARVE AND WATER WILL BECOME PRECIOUS. OH, AND DON'T FORGET YOUR FACTOR 99 SUN CREAM IF YOU'RE GOING OUTSIDE! GOODNIGHT!

Mayta wasn't going to go hungry. He was simply going to train his people to fight and go out and pinch the food and water from other tribes. He was going to be the biggest bully since Manco Capac.

It's not surprising, really. Stories say Mayta had grown up as a big, bad boy, picking fights with any boys he came

143

across. (You probably know someone like that.) He wasn't afraid to fight with bigger boys and the legends say he 'beat them badly'.

While he was still a boy he picked a fight with some peasants near Cuzco and killed them. This started a revolt by their tribe and his dad had trouble keeping it under control . . .

So mighty Mayta Capac was the perfect emperor to start conquering his next-door neighbours and making them hand over their hard-earned food supplies.

It was soon time to make Mayta a man. He had to go through the correct Incan ceremony . . .

Bye-bye boyhood
Do you know anyone who is growing into a man? Then instead of a birthday party or a school-leaver's do, why not give them a special treat? An Incan initiation! Follow these simple Incan rules to see your pal safely into the adult world . . .

MAKING IT INTO MANHOOD
(How to turn a boy into a man.)

You need: a llama, a sharp knife, a whip, a running track, a sling, a shield, a hard wooden club (called a 'mace'), a hole punch, a breechcloth (like a big boy's nappy) — and don't forget the boy!

1. First sacrifice your llama. (Sneak up behind the llama with your club. Club it to death, skin it and roast the meat.)

2. Offer the meat to the god of the sun.

YUM!

3. Strip the boy to the waist, give him the whip and let him whip himself to drive out his boyhood.

OW! AGH! OUCH! HOP IT, BOYHOOD!

4. Arrange a foot race around a running track so the new man can show his speed against the other men.

PUFF! PANT!

5. Give the new man his weapons — a sling, a shield and a club.

OOH, TA!

(Wipe the llama's blood off the club before you present it.)

6. Pierce the new man's ears so everyone can see at a glance he is no longer a boy.

OW! ME EARS!

7. Give him his new name and his breechcloth.

145

Lord number 5: Conquering Capac

Mayta Capac made his son, Capac Yupanqui, Lord of Cuzco . . . then Mayta died. Most lords named their oldest son to be the next ruler. Young Capac Yupanqui *wasn't* Mayta Capac's oldest son. What was wrong with Capac Yupanqui's older brother?

a) he was too thick

b) he was too ugly

c) he was too kind and gentle

AAAH! WHO'S A LOVELY LITTLE LLAMA THEN?

Answer: **b)** Yes, the poor lad took after his grandfather, Lloque, and was considered too ugly to be the Lord of the Incas. (Not like royals today! It seems they *have* to be ugly to get the job!)

Capac Yupanqui was the first Incan lord to capture lands outside the Cuzco Valley where the Incas started. But he only got about 12 miles from Cuzco. He wasn't exactly Julius Caesar or Alexander the Great, you understand.

Did you know . . . ?
Capac Yupanqui was known as the 'Unforgettable King' ... unfortunately we know very little about his reign. It seems that everyone has forgotten!

Lord number 6: Roca on – again!

Capac Yupanqui's son, Inca Roca, conquered a bit more to the south-east of Cuzco but the Incas weren't the greatest warriors, as the following story shows ...

Lord number 7: Huacac whack, whack!

Yahuar Huacac couldn't have hated his Ayarmaca captivity that much. He married an Ayarmaca girl! But then he also married other wives. Not a very healthy thing to do. Today, in most countries, marrying two women will get you punished. But in Incan times it was more deadly.

Yahuar Huacac announced …

And, would you believe it, the second wife arranged for the second son of the first wife to be murdered.

This was followed shortly after by the emperor's own death …

Lord number 8: Vicious Viracocha

Viracocha probably ruled around the early 1400s. He wasn't satisfied with being a 'lord' – he called himself 'Creator God'. (This is a bit like your head teacher calling themselves Minister of Education. A teeny bit over the top.)

Before Vile Vira came on the scene the Incas had attacked other tribes, conquered them, then gone home. Now Vira decided it was time they stayed there and ruled. First they

149

decided to take over the Ayarmaca people who lived to the south of the Incas' Cuzco valley. So what did they do?

Wrong! The Incas were smarter than you – that's why they got to rule Peru, which is more than you'll ever do. No, the Incas attacked the Urubamba! This was a valley beyond the Ayarmaca.

It worked. Whichever way the Ayarmaca faced they'd be stabbed in the back.

EVIL EMPERORS

The eight Incan lords had so far ruled only little Cuzco … and if that had been the end of the story you'd probably never have heard of them. But then they became more and more greedy. They wanted more land, more wealth, more people to push around. They weren't happy with a valley, or even a country. They wanted a whole empire. And, it was the next Incan lord, a lad called Pachacuti, who was the man for the job.

Did you know …?
Pachacuti got his name after a great battle victory. 'Pachacuti' means 'cataclysm' – or 'he who shakes the Earth'.

Pachacuti's date with fate: 1438
The Incas didn't get all their own way in bossing the Andes. Another people, the Chancas, to the west of the Incas, were getting pretty powerful. In 1438 the Chancas attacked first!

The Lord of Cuzco's son, Pachacuti Inca Yupanqui, defended their Cuzco home while his dad, Viracocha, went off with his other son, Urcon, to a safer fort near Calca. Now there were *two* Inca states – Pachacuti's and Viracocha's. But not for long. First Viracocha died.

Then Viracocha's other son Urcon got into a fight with Pachacuti's forces and was killed.

It left Pachacuti in charge.

Pach's pinching

Pachacuti defeated the Chanca attack thanks to a bit of luck. The Chancas took an image of their god into battle and Pach's warriors managed to capture it. The Chancas panicked and began to run away. They were massacred. Pach made the most of this victory and told a bit of a fib to make it sound more magical ...

The truth? As the Chancas ran away hundreds of Inca supporters, living in the hills, ran down and attacked them. Yes – the Chancas were massacred in the hills. But, no – the attackers weren't rocks!

Terror tactics

Pachacuti's big fib was widely believed. Enemies of the Incas were scared and the Incan warriors made the most of that fear. This is what they did …

1 Incan armies started to carry platforms into battle. On these platforms were piles of sacred stones.

Future enemies took one look at the pile of Incan rocks and gave up without a fight!

2 To add to the fear-factor the Incas took the defeated Chanca leaders and stuffed their skins with straw and ashes. The scarecrow corpses were taken to a special burial ground and seated on stone benches. The stuffed arms were bent so that when the wind blew the dead fingers beat the stretched skin on their bellies like drums! The message was clear …

3 The Incan warriors went into battle with war songs that were grisly and gruesome. Want to try one? Next time your history teacher gives you a dreadful detention then fight back with this ancient Incan chant …

Of course you couldn't *really* drink chicha from your teacher's skull because chicha is beer. You wouldn't want to get into trouble for under-age drinking, would you? Probably best if you just drink cocoa from the teacher's skull and stay out of trouble. (And no playing those bone flutes and skin drums when people are trying to get to sleep!)

Brotherly love
Pachacuti's warriors seemed unbeatable. The trouble was that Pach's younger brother, Capac Yupanqui, was having a great time invading neighbours and becoming a rich, powerful, popular general. Pach was worried.

154

What did he do? Well, if the Incas had a motto it would be, 'When in doubt, snuff them out!' So of course, Pachacuti had his brother murdered. Being the brother of an Incan emperor was a job for life – but sadly that life was often very short.

Pachacuti's sons went north and south conquering their neighbours and making the Incan Empire safe – safe for the Incas, that is.

Now Pachacuti could stop the fighting and enjoy a bit of ruling.

Pach's patch and Top Cat Topa

Pachacuti decided it was time for some changes and he had the power to make them. He had only taken over as emperor from his father after a lot of fighting and he didn't want that to happen when he died, so he made his son Topa Inca Yupanqui the next emperor, then retired.

Topa was topa the pops when it came to ruling and he and his dad made some nice new rules. If the Incas had been able to write, their laws may have read something like this ...

155

THE TEN INCA COMMANDMENTS

1. Cuzco will be the capital of the Incan Empire. The fortress of Sacsahuaman in Cuzco will be the strongest in the world.

2. The people will work on improving the Cuzco valley farms – levelling the earth and moving the river – so it will be the greatest food producer ever.

3. A dead emperor's lands will be shared out amongst his family. Each new emperor must conquer new lands of his own.

4. Conquered peoples will be scattered round other parts of the Incan Empire to work for the Incas – that will also stop them gathering together to revolt.

5. Girls of conquered tribes may become Chosen Women (Quechua Aclla Cuna) to serve in the Incan temples or be married off to great Incan soldiers.

6. A number of conquered men will be chosen to serve in the Incan Army.

7. Everyone will worship the Incan god, Viracocha. There will be priests, prayers and temples. All conquered peoples must worship Viracocha, and pay his priests with food and work. (But they can keep their old religion too.)

8. The emperor may marry his sister, but no other men may marry their sisters.

9. The emperor may marry as many women as he wishes, but no other man may. A chief minister may have 50 wives, an ordinary minister just 30 and the lower your class the fewer wives you may have.

10. If anyone wishes to speak to the emperor then he or she must take off their sandals and place a small load on their back as a sign of respect.

Imagine that in your country! First you're invaded and then you're …

- Split from your friends – all those mates who share the same jokes and support the same football team.
- Split from your sisters who are sent off to work in some distant temple or forced to marry some great national hero … like Prince Charles!
- Forced to work to pay for food that mostly goes to your enemy … like a vegetarian working in a butcher shop.

- Shipped off to another part of the invader's world where you don't know the language and live in a strange house. It could be anywhere … like Bournemouth, Blackpool or Buckie!
- Taught a new religion with new prayers and forced to worship a new god. It's a bit like being forced to support a new football team … like Bournemouth or Blackpool or Buckie Thistle!

The only good news is that the Incas will allow you to worship your old gods – as well as the new Incan ones.

Cheerless Chosen Women

Would you like to be an Incan 'Chosen Woman'? Sounds a bit special, doesn't it? If the Incas had advertised for Chosen Women they might have done it like this:

By the 1500s there were several thousand of these Chosen Women. Would you apply?

Apart from ending up as a temple sacrifice there was another danger in being a Chosen Woman ... You must never *ever* become pregnant. The punishment was pretty horrible ...

Amazingly there *was* one way that a Chosen Woman could avoid this terrible treatment. All she had to do was say ...

... and she would be free!

Rotten royal roads

Another thing the Incas could do with conquered peoples was force them to work on building the Incan 'Royal Roads'.

Four roads led from the four quarters of the Incan kingdom and they met in the middle of Cuzco. The Incas called their empire 'Tahuantinsuyu' – which, as you know, means 'The Four Quarters of the World'. The four Royal Roads were important.

160

So what? you ask! So *you* try building a path down your back garden without…

- iron (for tools like shovels and pick-axes).
- written words (for making plans and organizing work).
- wheels (so everything had to be dragged).
- money (so paying workers and supplying them with food was tricky over big distances).

The Incas had none of these things!

The roads were useful for a fast messenger service across the empire and to move Incan armies quickly when trouble broke out. The Spanish conquistador Pedro de Cieza de Leon described one road …

In human memory no highway is as great as this. It is laid through deep valleys and over high mountains, through snow banks and swamps, through live rock and along raging rivers. In some places smooth and paved, in others tunnelled through cliffs, skirting gorges, linking snow peaks with stairways and rest stops, everywhere clean-swept and litter-free, with taverns, storehouses, and temples of the sun.

The mountain roads had walls along the edge to stop you falling off the mountain. Very thoughtful, but a huge task to build hundreds of miles of walls. And doesn't it make you wonder who got the job of sweeping up the litter?

Marvellous messengers

The Incas had no way of writing things down (although they did have a clever recording system by tying knots in coloured string). Instead stories and messages were remembered.

There was no Postman Pat to carry letters around the Empire. Instead there was a relay-team of runners – the *chasqui*.

- These young men ran about a kilometre each to the next post and carried a message in their head. They then went back to their post and waited for the next message.

The chasqui chain were able to carry messages hundreds of miles across the Empire very quickly.

- The skill wasn't just in the running, but in the remembering. They had to get the messages exactly right, word for word. One word wrong and they would be punished – a bit like a history exam.
- The runners worked 15 days before they had some time off.

- They carried a badge to show they were servants of the emperor. They also carried a sling and a star-headed mace to defend themselves against wild animals.
- Messages were carried at around 150 miles a day – that's London to Cardiff if you want to look it up on a map.
- Messengers didn't just carry messages – they could be asked to carry food.

One emperor loved sea food and had it brought by messenger from the coast every day. If the fish wasn't fresh then the messenger was executed!

Did you know …?
The Incan armies marched north, south, east and west but they stopped at the edge of the Amazon rainforest. That rainforest was occupied by lowland tribes and many of them were head-hunters.

Wonder why they stopped there?

Horrible Huayna

Emperor Topa followed the trend of all the Incan emperors and died. (Around 1493 if you're interested in dates. Some people are, especially the sort you get in cakes.) He named son Huayna as next emperor … but then just before he died he said …

Huayna was a bit upset and his supporters murdered the guardian of young emperor Huari. Huayna got the throne he was supposed to have in the first place, so that was all right – unless you were Huari's guardian who got the chop, of course.

Remember, Incan emperors didn't get all their father's lands, which were shared out. A new emperor like Huayna had to go out and conquer more new land for himself. Huayna picked on the country we now call Ecuador, to the north.

He spent most of his reign battering Ecuador. In fact he liked it so much he thought he'd have a second capital city up there in Tumi Bamba. The lords back in Cuzco must have been shocked and horrified at the thought of a rival capital.

But before the Cuzco lords could revolt Huayna did a daft and deadly thing …

THEN A MESSAGE ARRIVED FROM CUZCO.

TELL ME YOUR MESSAGE WHILE I WIPE THESE LAST FEW REVOLTING PEOPLE OUT...

OH, DON'T MIND US...

DEAR EMPEROR HUAYNA,

HOPE THIS MESSAGE FINDS YOU WELL AND YOU ARE ENJOYING YOUR LITTLE BREAK UP THERE. I'M SURE YOU'RE DOING LOTS OF BLOOD-LETTING AND BUTCHERY TO KEEP THE PEASANTS IN THEIR PLACE.

ANYWAY, THINGS BACK HOME IN CUZCO ARE QUIET. VERY QUIET. NOW, DON'T GET TOO UPSET OR WORRIED, BUT THE REASON WHY THINGS ARE SO QUIET IS THE PEOPLE ARE DEAD OR DYING IN THEIR THOUSANDS, AND YOU DON'T GET MUCH QUIETER THAN A DEAD INCA.

IT SEEMS TO BE SOME SORT OF PLAGUE SWEEPING THE COUNTRY. IT'S COME FROM BOLIVIA. THE PEOPLE GO ALL FEVERISH AND SPOTTY AND DIE. LOTS OF THE WORKERS IN THE VALLEY ARE TURNING UP THEIR TOES AND HOPPING THE TWIG. IT'S JUST A MATTER OF TIME BEFORE THE PLAGUE REACHES

THE CITY AND I HATE TO THINK WHAT WILL HAPPEN THEN!

OF COURSE THE STUPID PEOPLE ARE PANICKING. THEY WANT TO SHUT THE CITY GATES AND KEEP THE PLAGUE OUT. THE TROUBLE IS, IF WE SHUT THE CITY GATES THEN WE KEEP THE FOOD OUT AND WE STARVE TO DEATH. AWKWARD, I'M SURE YOU'LL AGREE.

AS I SAY, IT'S NOT A HUGE PROBLEM AT THE MOMENT, BUT I THOUGHT YOU MIGHT LIKE TO KNOW. IF YOUR MIGHTY MIND CAN THINK OF AN ANSWER THEN PERHAPS YOU COULD LET US KNOW PRETTY DARN QUICK.

YOUR HUMBLE SERVANT,

GENERAL YASCA

TIPPY TOE

Yes, it's tough at the top. You get the throne but you also get the problems. What could unhappy Huayna do? What would you do? Only an idiot Inca would rush back to Cuzco, catch the plague and die! But that's what Huayna did! He died so quickly he didn't name the next emperor … so that started another Incan punch-up for the throne. Nothing new there then.

166

Did you know …?

Huayna's son died a few days after his dad from the same plague. That meant two half-brothers (Huascar and Atahuallpa) were left to fight one another for the throne. While they were fighting, the Incan Empire was divided – just as Spanish invaders arrived. That's what made it so easy for the Spanish to defeat them.

You could say the Spanish plague was the first attack which helped the conquistadors to win. Maybe as many as eight million of the twelve million Incas died before the Spanish arrived. Invisible germs were the best weapons the Spanish could ever have had! Which just goes to show, 'Coughs and sneezes spread diseases … and spread Spanish empires with eases!'

TOP OF THE CLASS

Incan people were told what they should be doing at each age and what they should be wearing … just like school. Only Incas never got to leave school the way you do.

Dire dress

Everyone had to wear what they were told. Each tribe had its own head-dress – and you were not allowed to pretend you were from another tribe by wearing their head-dress instead! You also had to dress the right way for your class – you couldn't be a peasant and dress too posh!

Peasant dress-sense
If you want to look like an Incan peasant here's how …

MEN   WOMEN

A LARGE CLOAK OVER THE SHOULDERS, TIED IN THE FRONT. (THE FINER THE CLOTH AND EMBROIDERY, THE HIGHER YOUR CLASS.)

A SLEEVELESS TUNIC

A BREECH-CLOTH

A SHOULDER MANTLE

A WRAPAROUND SKIRT THAT REACHED FROM BENEATH THE ARMS TO THE ANKLES, WITH THE TOP EDGES DRAWN OVER THE SHOULDERS AND FASTENED WITH STRAIGHT PINS.

A DECORATED SASH

Wee women

Girls! Now that you look like an Incan woman you need to dress your hair like the Incas. Here's how to do it …

1 Collect pee in a bucket. (Your family and friends can all chip in and help you fill that bucket fast.)

2 Leave the pee for a week to brew (the way beer is left to brew – except your pee won't end up tasting like brown ale).

3 Wash your hair by soaking it in the bucket of brewed pee. (This will get rid of the grease and leave your hair lovely and shiny – honest!)

4 When your hair is dry you can start making it into braids. To hold the hair in place wet it with some of that pee. (Hair spray hasn't been invented. Sorry.)

5 Find your Prince Charming and say …

Then hope that your Prince Charming likes a Cinderella who smells like a toilet!

Weather wizardry

The Incan family groups were called 'ayllu' and the head of a large family was called a 'curaca'. A curaca had power over

everyone in the family ... but you'd have to be crackers if you
wanted to be one of the curacas. Curacas took the complaints
from the family and went to the gods for help ...

WE COULD DO WITH A BIT OF RAIN. HOW ABOUT IF I SACRIFICE THIS LLAMA TO YOU?

When it worked the curaca was a hero ... but he also got the
blame when things went wrong. What would you do if your
garden was ruined by a drought?

A Spaniard described what happened to one clumsy
curaca ...

> *A powerful curaca called Fempellec was the ruler of his*
> *village. This lord moved the statue of a god from the*
> *temple. The villagers said that this made the gods angry*
> *and they sent a terrible drought. His people died. The*
> *priests then took Fempellec and drowned him.*

If there was a drought then how could they drown him? The
Spaniard didn't explain. Maybe they drowned him in a
dried-up river?

Would you kill your dad for a dried-up garden? (On
second thoughts you'd better not answer that!)

Mister masters

Men ruled Tahuantinsuyu. Women worked and had children
but had no power. A man, though, could increase his power

by having children. It was almost like a supermarket loyalty card – the more points you had the richer you were ... except instead of points you had children and wives.

THE TUZCO BONUS OFFER

MEN! TAKE THE INCA TRAIL TO POWER!
It's so simple!

JUST COLLECT THOSE KIDS AND WIN TERRIFIC TITLES

5 CUTE KIDS AND YOU'LL BE NAMED 'LITTLE OVERSEER'

FOR JUST 10 CHARMING CHILDREN WE'LL NAME YOU 'OVERSEER'

BUT GO FOR THE JACKPOT!

A MAN WITH A FABULOUS FAMILY OF 50 CAN BE LORD OF HIS OWN VILLAGE!

Yes! You too can be a cool Curaca. Start right now collecting the wonderful wives that will take you to the Tuzco Top!

Remember our motto:
THE MORE THE MERRIER!

More children meant more workers to produce more food and more power ... for the men.

Keeping in class

Now you are ready to live like an Inca. What you *did* each day depended on your age. The Incan laws told you exactly what you should be doing. They divided their people into 12 classes. If the Incas could have written their rules down they'd probably have looked something like this ...

1 **Babies** (in arms) and 2 **Infants** (up to one year): In the care of their parents.

3 **Children** (aged 1–9): Children aged 1–5 may play. Children aged 5–9 must help parents in small tasks. Girls must help mind the babies, cart water and animal feed, weed, and help the women make beer. At age 5 girls must start to learn how

to weave. Girls planning to be servants will be sent away to be trained.

4 Youths (aged 9–16): Boys to be trained as *llamamechecs* (llama herders of the llama herds). Girls aged 9–12 will gather flowers and herbs for the dyeing of textiles and for medicinal use. Girls aged 12–16 will work at home, keeping house and producing textiles (though some may serve as *llamamechecs*). Girls are allowed to marry at 14, although most will wait until they are 18.

5 **Young men** (aged 16–20) and 6 **Prime men** (aged 20–25): Will work as post-runners, as senior llama herdsmen to the *llamamechecs*, and as servants to military officers.

7 **Young women** (aged 18–30): Women are considered full adults at 18 (unlike men who will not become adults until 25). At this age they should be wives and mothers.

8 *Puric* (men 25–50): This age group of men should be married. At 25, they will be heads of households. They must learn to farm their given piece of land and pay taxes and serve in the army if they are called to. They might also be sent out to some remote part of the empire to pioneer it and to keep an eye on any hostile or disloyal natives in the area. Some men in this class are also called on to work in the state's mines.

9 **Unmarried women and widows** (women 30–50): They will make pottery and cloth, and work as house servants.

10 **Old men** (aged 50–60): These men are semi–retired and have no state or army duties. They are expected to help out from time to time during harvest and planting seasons, or to do light work as public officers, clerks, and storekeepers.

11 **Elders** (aged 60–80): Both men and women will eat, sleep, and may do light work if they are up to it, such as tending guinea pigs. They are pensioners and are tended to by the state.

12 **Invalids** (sick and disabled): They are expected to work as their disabilities allow, but are otherwise in the care of the state.

You'll notice there is no class at all for people over 80, so it seems not too many Incas made it that long! Imagine having your whole life planned for you by the government like this! Still, there was always death to look forward to.

Stinging school

You will also notice there's no school in there for you peasants. But if you were a lord's child then you would get four years of lessons …

INCAN SCHOOL TIMETABLE
YEAR 1: THE INCAN LANGUAGE (QUECHUA)
YEAR 2: RELIGION
YEAR 3: KNOTTED STRING (QUIPUS)
YEAR 4: HISTORY

Imagine! A whole year doing history! Horrible!

Of course you could make it more fun by messing about in lessons, but be warned! The punishment was pretty nasty …

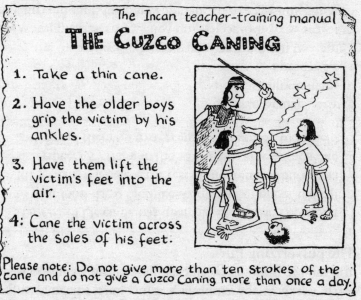

The Incan teacher-training manual

THE CUZCO CANING

1. Take a thin cane.

2. Have the older boys grip the victim by his ankles.

3. Have them lift the victim's feet into the air.

4. Cane the victim across the soles of his feet.

Please note: Do not give more than ten strokes of the cane and do not give a Cuzco Caning more than once a day.

And you thought being sent to do sums outside your head-teacher's door was nasty!

Shake, rattle and stroll

Of course the festivals would give you a few days off school. There would be a parade of men playing drums, tambourines, flutes and pototoes … no, not *potatoes*, dummy! The pototo was a large shell (called a conch) that was blown like a trumpet.

ONE POTOTO, TWO POTOTO, THREE POTOTO, FOUR...

When you went to the parade you could join the dancing and wear 'shaker bracelets' on your wrists and ankles. What would you use to make your rattling bracelets?

a) glass beads

b) small seashells

c) dried llamas' toenails

Answer: c) Dried llamas' toenails, of course. Pop along to your local llama sacrifice with a pair of pliers and rip the toenails out before the rest of the animal is burned as a sacrifice. Dry them in the sun, drill a hole in each one and thread them on to a string. You're ready to rattle!

The pulverizing Puric

You can see from the Incan class list that the men who went off to serve in the emperor's army were expected to be married at that age. This meant that the men had to leave their wives behind.

An old Incan legend, passed on by word of mouth, tells of the dramatic result of this on one family …

Once upon a time there was a young man, a Puric, who was sent for to serve as a soldier. He had to leave his young son and his wife.

'I will miss you both,' he sniffed.

'I'll miss you too,' his wife snivelled.

'And I'll mith you motht of all!' the little boy lithpt … I mean *lisped*.

When the Puric had left, his wife wept over her weaving and cried over her cooking and sobbed over her sewing. 'Don't cwy, Mummy!' the little boy said.

Suddenly a breeze blew a white butterfly through the window. 'It's a signal from my husband,' the woman whispered. 'So long as the butterfly visits I will know he is safe!'

'What dat?' her son said and pointed a podgy finger at the butterfly.

His mother sighed, 'It's my lover!'

And so they lived happily till the Puric returned. As it happened the little boy was pulling weeds in the garden so he was the first to see his father marching down the road. He ran on to the road and the Puric swept the boy up into his strong arms. 'My son! How have you been?'

'Gweat!' the little boy laughed.

The man stopped and put him down. 'Weren't you upset? Weren't you and Mummy lonely?' he gasped.

'No!' the little boy laughed. 'Mummy's lover came to thee her everwee day!'

The man picked up his mighty club, raced into the house and smashed his wife till she was a crushed corpse.

The little boy came in and saw the butterfly flutter round the head of his panting father. 'Look, Daddy!' he cried. 'Here is Mummy's lover, come to thee her!'

Live like a lord

It seems to have been much more fun to be an Incan emperor. Why not try it and find out what it was like? If you want to be Incan emperor (Sapa Inca) of your class then here's a quick guide …

You looking at me, mate?

The Sapa Inca is descended from the sun – a sort of sun son. No one can look at the sun, so no one can look at *you* directly. Wherever you go your subjects must look down … or else. When the lower classes want to speak to you they must turn their backs and bow to show respect. (Though someone turning and bowing may show their backside, which hardly shows respect!) At court the Sapa Inca often sat behind a screen.

Make your own screen

① Take one old door.
② Nail planks to base.
③ Attach label.

DON'T LOOK AT ME OR YOU'LL GO BLIND. TURN YOUR BACK AND BOW

Atahuallpa spoke from behind a screen to his brother who passed on the messages like a walking cordless telephone.

Tassel hassle

It's no use being an emperor if you don't let people know you're in charge. As Sapa Inca you wear a special fringe *not* a crown. On your head-dress you wear a fringe of red, woollen tassels hung from little gold tubes.

How to make a Sapa Inca head-dress

① Cut straws in half and paint them gold.

② Thread through red wool to leave tassels at one end.

③ Stick the tasseled tubes to a headband.

GOLD

Tinge that fringe

Pick your heir – the favourite son of yours who will take the throne when you die or decide to retire. Your heir wears his hair under a fringe that's tinged bright yellow. (Try saying that with a mouthful of mushy peas!) He also has a stick with a feather on it that sticks out 10 cm from his forehead.

Plug that lug

Pierce your ears. Male members of the Incan royal family and nobles of pure Incan blood wore huge earplugs (earrings that stretch pierced ears). Unlike anyone else in the empire they cropped their hair. The size of hole in your ear shows how noble you are; the larger the hole, the more noble the wearer. A conquistador said ...

> *He who had the largest ears was held to be the finest gentleman.*

Francisco Pizarro, the Spaniard who came and conquered the Incas, was amazed to see that the Incan king had earlobes that hung to his shoulders and that the ear discs worn by some Incan nobles were as large as oranges. You could try this short cut to emporer-sized ear-lobes ...

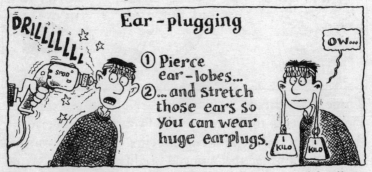

Perhaps the strangest custom of all was for the royal family to fit earplugs ... to their llamas!

Nibble your nosh

The Incas didn't have tables. They ate off cloths on the floor. But you are an emperor! We can't have that.

- First, sit on your throne – a curved piece of wood about 20 cm high.
- Send everyone else out of the room – because a Sapa Inca always eats alone.
- Now clap your hands and your serving women will bring in your food – they will stand there, holding the plates while you eat from them.

But there is one Sapa Inca habit you probably shouldn't try at home – or in your school dinner hall. A conquistador said …

If the emperor coughed or spat, a woman held out her hand and he spat into her palm. And any hairs that fell from his head on to his clothes were picked up by the women and eaten. The reason for these customs is known; the spitting was a royal thing to do; the hairs because he was afraid of being bewitched.

Yeuch!

Pick up that litter

As Sapa Inca you are too grand to walk. You will be carried everywhere in a 'litter'.

The holes in the side let the air in and let the emperor see out, but peasants can't see in. Why not train 20 strong and steady litter-carriers and go for a quick run down the motorway? Your wives and your treasure can follow on in hammock-litters.

LIVE LIKE AN INCA

Crime time

There was very little crime in Tahuantinsuyu because everyone shared what they owned so there was no point in stealing. But what would happen to a man who murdered his wife? Well, for a start, he would NOT be locked in prison.

There were three main crimes to be punished: murder, insulting the emperor, and insulting the gods. The punishment for these was death and the Incas had a nice simple way to execute someone. What was it?

a) They would cut the criminal to pieces and feed them to the guinea pigs.
b) They would drown the criminal in Lake Titicaca.
c) They would throw the criminal off a cliff.

Answer: c) Which would you prefer?

A rare, but really serious crime was to have one of the emperor's wives as a girlfriend. The punishment was to be stripped naked, tied to a wall and left to starve to death.

Smaller crimes had lesser punishments – nice little things like having hands or feet chopped off or eyes gouged out! (The criminal could see the point of the punishment ... but then not much else!)

Particular punishments

We have 'set' punishments for some crimes today. So a motorist who drives 10 miles an hour above the speed limit will be fined a set amount and have 'penalty points' put on his or her driving licence. The Incas didn't have money so they didn't have fines and they didn't have driving licences … possibly because they had no paper. But they did have 'set' punishments for certain crimes.

Could you be a law enforcer in Tahuantinsuyu? Match the crime to the powerful punishment …

FOR THE CRIME OF...

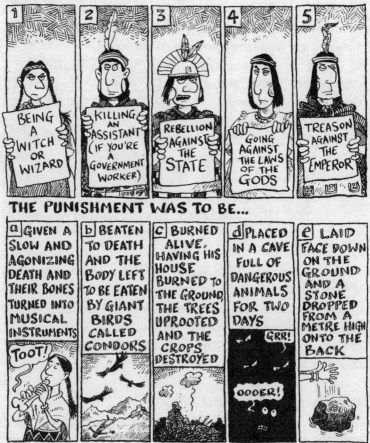

1. BEING A WITCH OR WIZARD
2. KILLING AN ASSISTANT (IF YOU'RE A GOVERNMENT WORKER)
3. REBELLION AGAINST THE STATE
4. GOING AGAINST THE LAWS OF THE GODS
5. TREASON AGAINST THE EMPEROR

THE PUNISHMENT WAS TO BE...

a) GIVEN A SLOW AND AGONIZING DEATH AND THEIR BONES TURNED INTO MUSICAL INSTRUMENTS

TOOT!

b) BEATEN TO DEATH AND THE BODY LEFT TO BE EATEN BY GIANT BIRDS CALLED CONDORS

c) BURNED ALIVE, HAVING HIS HOUSE BURNED TO THE GROUND THE TREES UPROOTED AND THE CROPS DESTROYED

d) PLACED IN A CAVE FULL OF DANGEROUS ANIMALS FOR TWO DAYS

GRR!

OOOER!

e) LAID FACE DOWN ON THE GROUND AND A STONE DROPPED FROM A METRE HIGH ONTO THE BACK

EEEK!

In the cave of Sancay, prisoners convicted of treason were placed in a cavern full of wild animals, toxic toads, and venomous reptiles. If a convict survived two days in these surroundings he was pardoned and released, since his survival seemed to signal that he was obviously under the protection of the gods.

5d) A conquistador described this punishment …

4c) Seems a bit cruel to punish the trees! Maybe they just picked ash trees to match the ash owner!

3a) It's nice to think that, after you are dead, your bones will give people so much pleasure, isn't it?

2e) This sometimes killed the prisoner. If it didn't then he was left with severe injuries for the rest of his life.

Answers: **1b)** … witch is not very pleasant.

Foul food

Beastly beer

When the Incas had a festival they enjoyed large amounts of their 'chicha' beer. It's probably more fun to watch llamas being slaughtered when you've had a few pints!

Do you have a school assembly you have to go to? Need a cup or two of chicha to give you strength? Then follow these simple (but disgusting) Incan instructions …

On the other hand you may prefer to stick to lemonade – without the spit.

Tasty tatties

The Incas ate lots of potatoes. One of their words for these vegetables was 'papa' which Spanish invaders changed a little to give us the modern word 'potato'. But the Incas and the tribes they conquered had over 200 other words for potatoes! (I wonder who counted them?)

We only have about a dozen …

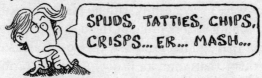

SPUDS, TATTIES, CHIPS, CRISPS… ER… MASH…

The Incas even had dried potatoes long before they appeared in your local supermarket. They picked their potatoes in the autumn when the Andes days were warm and the nights fell below freezing. Then they'd …

- spread the potatoes on the ground overnight to freeze
- let them thaw the next morning
- gather them into large piles in the afternoon
- trample them under their bare feet to squeeze out the water
- spread out the pulp to dry
- store it over the winter months
- add water whenever they fancied some spuds – just like today's packets of dried potato.

The potato crop, like the rest of the Incan farm food, was divided into three equal parts …

- one for the village
- one for the stores in case of famine
- one for the priests to burn as a gift to the gods.

Wood was scarce in some parts of the Andes so how did you roast your potatoes? Over a fire of dried llama droppings, of course! (Well, you enjoy Smoky Bacon crisps – why not Roast Llama Dropping flavour?)

SCRUNCH SCRUNCH SCRUNCH YECH!

ACTUALLY THE LLAMA DROPPINGS TASTE BETTER!

Terrible treatments

The Incas were fairly healthy with no plague-type diseases – until the conquistadors brought them as a special gift from Spain! But they did have some sicknesses ... and some ways to treat them that your local doctor would probably not advise today ...

Cuzco Cures

Reliable remedies for ill Incas

Wicked wounds: Got a nasty llama bite? Been stabbed or stoned by an enemy warrior? Simply take the bark from a pepper tree, boil it in water and slap it on the wound. It's hot stuff for curing wounds is the pepper tree.

Dreadful diarrhoea: Take the leaves from the coca plant and chew them. These wonderful leaves also help lessen your hunger and stop you feeling sick when you climb those high mountains.

Awful aches: Take a glass knife and gouge a hole between your eyes. This will cure your headache in no time! Or if the pain is in your arm then let out arm blood – you'll see that there's no 'arm in it!

188

Hot tots: If baby has a fever then collect the family pee in a pot and wash baby in the lovely liquid. If that doesn't work then give it to baby to drink! Yummy drink from Mummy!

Ill infants: All sensible mothers cut their baby's umbilical cord when it's born then dry it and store it. When the child falls sick just give it the umbilical cord to suck on and it will suck the pain and evil spirits from its body!

Horrible headaches: Draw an oval on the skull then drill holes along it about a quarter centimetre each. Lift out the bone and let out the evil spirits from the head. Another way is to saw two lines at right angles. Of course the patient would like plenty of coca leaves to drug them while you do this! There's nothing like a hole in the head to drain the pain!

It seems that the hole-in-the-head treatment worked. Archaeologists have found skulls with these pieces removed and it is clear the wound healed and the patient survived.

Village healers also used a special trick to make sick people believe they were cured. First they fed the patient black and white corn flour then hypnotized them into a trance. While the family watched, the healer pretended to open up the

patient's stomach with a knife. He would then appear to pull out a nasty collection of snakes, toads and other objects. (Naturally this was a conjuring trick.) They then cleaned the blood off the body and said, 'Look! The wound is healed and all this poison inside you is gone!'

The patient would feel better because they really *believed* they'd been cured.

Brush up your appearance

Boys! There's nothing a girl hates more than rotten teeth and bad breath. So why not make sure your teeth are clean the Incan way? Here's how …

1 Take some molle twigs (from the South American pepper tree – the garden hedge will NOT do).

2 Roast the twigs over a hot fire till the ends are smoking.

3 Place the hot roast twig against your gums.

A conquistador described what happened next …

The twigs scald the gums, the burnt flesh falls off to reveal new flesh underneath. This new flesh is very red and healthy!

Now, lads, go out and find your dream girl. With luck she will be a cannibal who enjoys kissing a lad who tastes of roasted human flesh.

HORRIBLE HISTORIES HEALTH WARNING
Do not try this! A baboon's bum is red and healthy but you wouldn't want it in your mouth! Remember, smoking can damage your health … and so can putting a smoking twig into your mouth.

Funny money

The Incas didn't use money. They exchanged their work for what they wanted. Good idea for school …

CLEAN THE BLACKBOARD AND YOU GET A BAR OF CHOCOLATE!

WHAT DO I GET IF I CLEAN THE TOILET?

SMELLY HANDS

They also used materials and clothing as a sort of money. Not such a good idea …

It isn't as if a sort of money hadn't been invented. The Sican people (conquered by the Incas) used copper axe-heads as coins. You can make these yourself and be the richest Sican in your class. All you need is half a tonne of sheets of copper and a big hammer. Cut and hammer the copper into axe-head shapes. Each one is about 5 cm long by 3 cm wide.

Rich Sican lords were buried with up to 500 kg of these axe-heads, stacked up in piles of 500 around them. Sican lords were also buried with up to twenty human sacrifices.

The Incas never copied the idea of copper-axe money, which may not be a bad thing. After all, the Bible says the love of money is the root of all evil. So maybe the Incas simply decided the copper axe-coins were just axing for trouble!

Funnier money

Another reason the Incas had no money may be to do with the way they *thought*. So, you and your parents and the people in your country *think* …

… but an Inca would think …

The conquistadors never really understood this. An Incan lord would have lots of wives so he could have lots of children and grandchildren – that would make him 'rich'. The Spanish were horrified and wanted to hang an Incan lord, Don Juan, because he had lots of wives.

Don Juan tried to save his life in two ways …

1 Don Juan gave a fortune in buried treasure to the Spanish officer who wanted him executed. It was valuable to the Spaniard, but not to Don Juan.

2 The Spanish officer said, 'Send your extra wives to the home of a good Christian woman to learn Christianity.' Don Juan sent the Incan women ... but cheated and kept his favourite extra wife at home. He sent another woman in her place.

Sadly the Spanish discovered the bribery and the trickery. Don Juan was very quickly hanged ... for doing what his ancestors had always done.

Inca Inquisition

Have you noticed how teachers like to ask you questions? Why do they bother when they probably know the answers?

It's time to turn the tables and torment your teacher with this simple quiz. If they get less than 5 out of 10 they are probably ready for early retirement. If they get more than 5 out of 10 then they were probably around in Incan times and are ready for retirement anyway! Answer true or false ...

1 When an Inca became too old to work they were turned into a mummy and buried ... even if they weren't dead!

THIS IS NO WAY TO TREAT YOUR MUMMY!

2 Old people were given the job of collecting lice.

3 Inca Huaca was released by the people who captured him because he cried.

4 Atahuallpa's leading general, Chalcuchinma, had his legs burned to a crisp to get him to reveal Incan treasure stores.

194

5 Emperor Atahuallpa's chair carriers gave up when the Spanish chopped off their hands.

SORRY LADS — I'M GOING TO HAVE TO LET YOU GO.

6 Modern Peruvian men have mock sling fights in memory of their Incan ancestors, but no one gets hurt.

7 The Incan warriors were expert archers.

8 The Incas enjoyed popcorn.

9 The Incas ate dogs.

FANCY SOME POPCORN?

NO THANKS, I'M HAVING A HOT DOG!

10 The Incas rode on llamas.

Answers:

1 False. The Incas were among the first people to look after their old people. They had the first old age pensions – food supplies not money, of course. Some of the emperor's wealth was set aside for widows, orphans, old people and the disabled. The emperor's collectors took more food and materials than they needed, then they stored it in case there was a drought or a famine. (A bit like the way you save in a piggy bank. But, being from the Andes they probably had guinea-piggy banks!) The blind were given the task of picking seeds out of cotton plants and were paid with food and shelter.

2 True. When you were too old to farm you went to the Incan food store and you collected your old-age food pension. This was usually at the age of fifty. (Nowadays you get a bus pass at sixty and that's all – and they taste terrible.) But the old were expected to make themselves useful. Collecting firewood … and collecting lice. You then took your collection of lice to the leader of your family group.

LICE TO MEET YOU.

3 True. But Huaca had an incredible talent … he cried tears of blood! His captors were so amazed they set him free. (Don't try it yourself or you'll make a right mess of this book.)

4 True. But don't feel too sorry for the general. His favourite sport was drinking from the skulls of dead enemies. He survived the charred legs to go on and poison the emperor who took Atahuallpa's place. Not a nice man.

GRRR!

5 False. It is TRUE that they had their hands chopped off … but they did NOT give up their work, carrying Atahuallpa around the country! They carried the covered chair (litter) on their shoulders until they bled to death. (Maybe they carried on because they were devoted servants – or maybe because the Incas had a law against dropping their litter!)

6 False. The men from rival regions fight one another like knights fighting for the love of beautiful girls. These are mock fights yet every year several men get themselves killed.

7 False. The warriors preferred to use stones fired from slings. They didn't use bows and arrows because good wood for bows doesn't grow in the Andes.

8 True. Corn was their main food and they ate it toasted, boiled or ground into flour and baked. They also heated it till it 'popped'. Pity they didn't invent the cinema to go with the popcorn.

9 False. The Incas conquered the Huanca tribe and the Huanca loved to eat dog as a special treat. The Incas were a bit disgusted by this. They much preferred to eat guinea pigs (roasted or in a stew). The little furry friends ran around the house like pets till they were wanted for dinner. The Incas also ate llama meat (tastes a bit like mutton) but generally not much meat at all.

HERE FLUFFY! DINNER TIME!

10 False. Llamas were used like donkeys to carry loads but the Incas never rode them. Probably because the llamas have a nasty habit of stopping and sitting down for hours on end if they are overloaded or upset! The Incas were also wary of the llamas' greatest skill – spitting a long way, with a great aim, at anything (or anyone).

THE CRUEL CONQUEST

By 1532 the Incas had conquered dozens of states and ruled over 12 million people who spoke at least 20 different languages. Their empire stretched 2,000 miles from north to south and 500 miles east to west.

But the Spanish had discovered America thanks to Christopher Columbus. They smashed the Aztecs in Central America then they began to march south, looking for treasure. The Incas were attacked by Spanish invaders – all 250 of them! (Oh, all right, 198 soldiers and 62 horsemen if you want to be picky.)

So the Incas outnumbered the Spanish about 60,000 to 1. No contest?

Timeline

1526 Francisco Pizarro from Spain lands on the coast of Peru and is welcomed by the rich Incas. He is given lots of gold – he'll be back for more, of course. Next time he'll have an army!

1527 Emperor Huascar, one of Huayna's sons, takes the throne. His half-brother, Lord Atahuallpa, decides to fight him for it. Atahuallpa wins and captures Huascar.

1532 Pizarro and his little army arrive back in Peru and meet the young emperor Atahuallpa. The Spanish kidnap Atahuallpa and hold him to ransom. Many Incas believe

the Spanish could be fair-skinned gods. They don't fight.

1533 The Incas pay Atahuallpa's ransom, but the Spanish execute him anyway. That is a very sneaky thing to do. End of Incan Empire and the start of Peru's suffering.

1537 Incan rebel Manco Capac II sets up a new Incan kingdom at Vilcabamba. It can't last.

1541 Pizarro is assassinated ... not by the Incas though. This is a seriously unpopular bloke.

1572 The last Incan rebel stronghold is captured and emperor Tupac Amaru, son of Manco, is beheaded. Without a head the new Incan Empire is finished – and without a head Tupac Amaru isn't too grand either!

1600 For every hundred Incas alive when the Spanish arrived there are now only ten. Slavery and diseases from Europe have almost wiped them out in seventy years.

1782 Tupac Amaru II, descendant of last Incan emperor, leads a revolution against Spanish rule ... and fails. The Spanish make him watch the executions of his wife and sons, then they hang, draw and quarter him. (And you thought the Incas were cruel?)

SORRY, I MEANT, GIVE US A BIG PILE OF GOLD *AND* THE EMPEROR GETS THE CHOP!

POO!

NICE ONE! CAN WE HAVE A GO!

WE'VE WON BY A SHORT HEAD!

HANG ON... I'M THE ONE WHO'S MEANT TO BE REVOLTING!

1808 South American countries begin to rebel against Spanish rule. **1824** The Spanish are defeated and new countries are formed. In the old Incan homeland the country of Peru is set up.

Peculiar Peru

The Incas said they lived in Tahuantinsuyu. So, how come the Spanish arrived and called it Peru? Here's how …

The Spanish landed on the east coast of America. In 1511 the Spanish conquistador, Balboa, was weighing some gold when a young Amerindian chieftain struck the scales with his fist and said …

I CAN TELL YOU OF A LAND WHERE GOLD IS AS CHEAP AS IRON IS TO YOU. THEY EAT FROM GOLDEN PLATES AND DRINK FROM GOLDEN CUPS!

Then the Spanish heard stories of 'The Golden Man' – a South American king who was so wealthy he covered himself in gold dust every morning before he took a bath in his holy lake.

WHERE CAN WE FIND THIS GOLDEN MAN?

BIRU

The Incas were doomed from that moment. It took the Spanish twenty years to find 'Peru'. But once conquistador Pizarro arrived the Incas had had their chips. (Pizza and chips have always gone well together.)

Powerful Pizarro

The leading conquistador in Tahuantinsuyu was the Spaniard Francisco Pizarro (or Franny to you and me). With his 260 men he conquered millions of Incas. Who was this Pizarro? Some sort of Superman? Here are some terrible truths …

Franny's fantastic facts

1 Franny grew up in Spain as a poor boy whose job was to look after the pigs. That's where he first learned to bring home the bacon.

2 It is said that his parents ran away and left him. He survived because he was brought up by a sow!

3 Franny never learned how to write (the sow never taught him). He couldn't even write his own name and it was needed on the official documents. So what did Franny do? He had a stencil made of his name and coloured it in when he needed to sign a paper!

4 Franny joined the explorer Nunez de Balboa when he crossed Panama and discovered the Pacific Ocean in 1513. Balboa was beheaded by the king's trusted general, Pedrarias Davila. Franny wasn't daft and he became a follower of Davila and kept his head.

5 Franny then joined up with the soldier Diego de Almagro and they set off to conquer lands south of Panama. The people of Panama couldn't believe anyone could take such a risk – they nicknamed Almagro and Pizarro's little army 'the band of lunatics'. The Panama people were right; Franny came back with just a little gold – and left behind a lot of dead soldiers.

6 On his next expedition into South America Franny was wounded by arrows seven times but carried on.

Franny and 250 Spanish soldiers retreated to the safety of an island where he made a famous speech. He drew a line in the sand and said ...

> *Gentlemen, this line is work, hunger, thirst, weariness and sickness. If you wish to join me in facing these perils then cross the line and stand beside me like true friends. No matter how few there are, I know that we will be victorious!*

Would you cross the line? How many of those 250 gallant Spanish men crossed Franny's line? Was it ...

a) 13?
b) 113?
c) 213?

Answer: a) Just 13 swallowed this brave talk and joined him. He must have felt a bit of a twit!

7 Like all great leaders Franny had a lot of luck. One of his 'Glorious Thirteen' was a giant of a man called Pedro de Candia. This man offered to explore the trail ahead alone. He said ...

> *If I'm killed you will only have lost one man which is not important. But if I succeed your glory will be great!*

De Candia carried a metre-long wooden cross and marched towards the Incan town of Tumbez. It's said the Tumbez councillors released the Emperor's lion and tiger on to the path. The creatures weren't hungry and lay down at de Candia's feet. He patted them on the head and the people of Tumbez were gobsmacked. Or god-smacked. They were sure de Candia had come from the sun god and worshipped him.

HE'S CONQUISTADORABLE!

8 Peru was peppered with Pizarros. Franny's three brothers helped him to conquer the country. None of the brothers lived happily ever after. One, Hernando, went back to Spain and was locked in prison for 20 years for his great work! He was released and died at the age of 100 in terrible poverty.

Plotting Pizarro
The Spanish arrived in Tahuantinsuyu looking for gold. The King of Spain had given them ships and paid the Spanish soldiers. In return he wanted South American gold. Lots of it. Lots and lots and lots of it.

Exam time for teacher. Ask your history teacher, 'Can you answer each of these questions in just two words …?' (Of course they'll fail! Teachers can never use two words when two hundred will do!)

Franny Pizarro may not have been able to read and write … but at least he could answer these horrible historical challenges. Could you?

Question 1: How did a handful of Spanish conquistadors defeat the vast numbers of Incan warriors?

Answer: They cheated.

Pizarro led his men into the city of Cajamarca – the Incas thought this might have been a visit from some wandering gods and didn't try to resist.

Then Pizarro sent a message to Emperor Atahuallpa ...

Pizarro then had his cannon hidden covering the square and horsemen in the side streets. The Incas had never seen a cannon or a horse before. When Atahuallpa's bodyguard marched into the square the cannon opened fire and the horsemen rode in to finish them off. Up to seven thousand were butchered and Atahuallpa was taken prisoner. It makes those Spanish soldiers sound like brave but heartless killers. Yet Pedro Pizarro, who was there, said ...

While they waited for the signal many Spaniards wet their pants from terror without noticing it.

Pizarro may sound like a ruthless and cruel villain. But then Atahuallpa's plan had been to capture the Spanish, sacrifice some of them to the gods and turn the others to slaves ... after cutting off their naughty bits. Pizarro just got his attack in first!

Question 2: How did Pizarro get the Incan wealth from all corners of the 2,000 mile empire?

EASY PEASY!

Answer: Ransom Atahuallpa.

That way you get the Incan people to bring their treasure to you! Pizarro had Emperor Atahuallpa locked in a cell. He simply said …

IF YOU WANT YOUR EMPEROR BACK, THEN I WANT THE CELL FILLED WITH GOLD!

The Incas, incredibly, agreed. They brought 13,265 pounds of gold (6,017 kilos, give or take a nugget). They also brought 26 pounds (12 kilos) of silver. I guess that was their small change. It took the Incas eight months to bring all the treasure to the city.

Question 3: How did Pizarro make sure Atahuallpa didn't destroy him once the ransom was paid?

HMM...

Answer: Kill Atahuallpa.

Oh, yes, I know the Incas imagined their Emperor would be set free once the ransom was paid. But Pizarro wasn't daft. He never planned to let Atahuallpa go.

He said to Atahuallpa, 'We will burn you to death!'

That upset the Emperor a bit because he wanted his body to be turned into a mummy after death … and it's a bit hard to make anything out of ashes (unless it's an ashtray, of course).

Pizarro made a deal. 'Tell you what, Atty, old man. If you agree to become a Christian then I'll be really kind to you and have you strangled instead!'

Atahuallpa agreed.

The Emperor was tied to a stake, a cord was placed round his throat and tightened by twisting a stick until he was strangled – a cheerful little execution method called the garrotte.

IT'S NO CHOKING MATTER!

Of course Atahuallpa didn't mind too much … he was sure he'd be reborn again! Emperors didn't die, they just found a new body!

The Incan armies were lost without their leader and the small group of conquistadors easily took control. Pizarro had just one problem … and it wasn't with the Incas …

Awful Almagro

The trouble with being a great success is that some people will get jealous and hate you. If you want to be popular then be a failure and everyone will love you! The man who hated Franny Pizarro more than anyone was fellow Spanish conquistador, Diego de Almagro.

- Almagro and Pizarro conquered Tahuantinsuyu between them but Pizarro was the Spanish King's pet and Almagro got jealous.
- Almagro was sent south to help conquer Chile. Not only did he fail, but the Incas in Cuzco rebelled while he was away.
- When Almagro returned to fight the rebels he turned to Pizarro's brothers for help … but they refused to obey his orders during the fighting.
- Almagro put the brothers in prison and Pizarro was not a happy bunny.

- Spaniard fought Spaniard as Pizarro attacked Almagro. When Pizarro captured his old friend he showed Almagro the same mercy he'd shown to Atahuallpa. He had him strangled in the same way – then had his head cut off just to make sure!

Getting it In-ca neck

Almagro's expedition to Chile was a disaster because he made some daft mistakes. For a start he set off over the mountains in winter. Even the tough Incan helpers froze to death. Almagro set out with 12,000 Incas and 10,000 died in that first winter.

The Incas were chained together in long lines with iron collars around their necks ...

When an Inca fell sick it would take a long time, with frozen fingers and cold keys, to unfasten that collar. Almagro came up with a quick way of removing the Inca from the neck collar so the march wasn't held up for long. What was Almagro's short cut?

Answer: He chopped off the Inca's head.

Almagro wasn't the only conquistador to fail in Chile. The next conquistador to return to Chile, Pedro de Valdivia, who tried to take over the region in the 1550s, died when the Indians poured molten gold down his throat, saying,

You came for gold, now we give you all the gold you can use.

Franny's finale

Franny was killed by Almagro's son and his Spanish friends in the end, not by the Incas. He had built himself a palace in Lima and that's where they got him. But he went down fighting. He killed two of his attackers and then they came up with a wonderful plan – they threw one of their mates at Pizarro's sword! (Nice friendly thing to do!) As Pizarro tried to pull his sword out of this third corpse they stabbed him in the throat.

Franny died a Christian. He dipped a finger in the blood from his throat and made the sign of a cross on the floor. He kissed the bloody cross … then the last blows rained down on him. Plenty of people went to the funeral but no one cried. The leader of the assassins, Almagro's son, got the chop a year later.

Awesome Atahuallpa

It's easy to say, 'Aw! Poor Atahuallpa! Tricked and murdered. It's not fair!' But the truth is Atahuallpa took the throne from his half-brother with trickery and murder ... so perhaps he got what he deserved!

Atahuallpa ruled in the north – Atahuallpa had been his dad's favourite so Dad gave him a region of his own before he died. But that made the new Emperor (Atahuallpa's brother Huascar) nervous. First Atahuallpa promised to obey the Emperor ...

I WILL SEND YOU SERVANTS FROM MY REGION TO DO YOU HONOUR!

He sent the best soldiers he had, armed to the teeth! By the time Huascar realized this was actually an invading army it was too late. He was captured and his guards slaughtered in front of his eyes.

Atahuallpa wasn't finished ...

I WANT ALL OF HUASCAR'S MINISTERS AND CAPTAINS TO GATHER TOGETHER TO MAKE NEW LAWS! THEY WILL BE SAFE!

When they arrived he had them all put to death! That left the main danger lying in Atahuallpa's royal family – his 200 or so brothers and cousins.

I WANT THEM SACRIFICED! I WANT THEM HANGED, OR THROWN INTO A LAKE WITH STONES AROUND THEIR NECKS, OR THROWN FROM A CLIFF... AND YOU CAN LET HUASCAR WATCH THE FUN!

That should do it, eh? No. The women and children of the royal family had to go next. They were starved and then hung by the neck or the waist and left to die. (A Spanish writer said they were hung 'in ways too disgusting to mention' … so we won't mention them.)

Enough, Atahuallpa? Nope! The servants and water-carriers and gardeners and cooks were massacred too. In some cities just one man remained for every ten women.

Now he was safe from his half-brother. The trouble was he had weakened his fighting men when the threat came from the Spanish invaders.

Awfully big mistake, Atahuallpa!

The men with soft swords
Atahuallpa had defeated Huascar when he heard about the strangers who had arrived. He also heard about their guns, swords and horses – the things that would defeat him.

But the Incan generals didn't want to scare Atahuallpa so they told him a few little fibs …

> THEY HAVE THESE THINGS CALLED 'GUNS' – BUT THEY CAN ONLY STRIKE TWICE AND THEN THEY'RE FINISHED!

> THEY HAVE THESE STICKS CALLED 'SWORDS' – BUT THEY ARE AS SOFT AND HARMLESS AS A WOMAN'S WEAVING STICK!

> THEY HAVE THESE CREATURES CALLED 'HORSES' – BUT THEY ARE POWERLESS TO MOVE AT NIGHT!

> NOTHING TO FEAR THEN, CHAPS! LET'S MEET THEM AT SUNSET AND WE'LL BE FINE!

They did … and they weren't! When Atahuallpa arrived a priest explained the Christian religion to the Emperor … in Latin! He handed Atahuallpa a Bible … but the Emperor didn't even know what a book was! Not surprisingly, Atahuallpa was bored with the sermon and threw the Bible down. That was when the hidden conquistadors struck. A Spaniard wrote …

> *It was a wonderful thing to see. To see so great a lord as Atahuallpa, who came with such power, taken prisoner in so short a time.*

The writer also enjoyed the fact that while thousands of Incas were killed, not one conquistador died.

While Atahuallpa was imprisoned he didn't forget his brother Huascar. He sent out secret orders to have Huascar killed!

Silvery suffering

The Incan peasants had worked for their leaders and in return their leaders had cared for them. But the Spanish conquistadors made the Incan peasants work with just enough to keep them alive.

The greatest suffering was in the silver mines. The Spanish back in Spain were desperate for money (to pay soldiers to fight wars). The silver mine at Potosi was discovered and the Spanish worked the Incas to death to get its treasures.

Yet it wasn't the Spanish who discovered the mine. It was a llama herder. The story goes like this …

The shaking mountain was probably a small earthquake.

That old story of angry gods didn't bother the Spanish when they heard it. In 1571 they started mining for the silver and paid the workers with what?

a) pieces of the silver

b) pieces of farmland

c) pieces of cloth

Answer: **c)** The Spanish gave cloth to the chiefs who shared it out among the Incan mine workers. Imagine your teachers being paid in cloth!

So many Incas suffered in those mines they must have wished that herder had kept his mouth shut.

Working woes

The Spanish found new ways to make money from the Incas and brought them new ways to die …

- In the silver mines the workers would sweat to fill their cloaks with rocks then drag them to the surface. When they reached the cold air at the top of the mine they were chilled and many caught pneumonia and died.
- In the mercury mines the mercury could be breathed in with the dust and could poison the miners. It gave them raw throats, fever and a slow death.
- In the sugar-cane factories the Spanish brought in heavy machines to crush the sugar cane. They often ended up with crushed Incan peasants as well.

Routed rebels

Of course the Incas tried to rebel against Spanish rule from time to time. Not very successfully. They not only failed but suffered terribly.

During Manco Capac's Easter Uprising, in 1536, Spanish soldiers came towards the city to put down the uprising, and the Incan fighters taunted the Europeans by lifting their bare legs at them! (The insult is still used in the Andes.) Insulting, perhaps – but not very effective!

The battle raged for over a month. The Spanish tried terror tactics: they chopped up Indian women and cut off the right hands of captive warriors to toss them out of their fortress for the Indians to find.

After the Cuzco uprising, Pizarro first tried to befriend Manco Capac. That failed, so the Conquistador had Manco's sister–wife …

- stripped
- tied to a tree
- whipped with rods
- shot to death with arrows.

Then her corpse was put in a basket and floated downstream into the Incan camp.

Pizarro also burned alive Manco's best general and 15 other important Incan captains.

Manco thought he'd made friends with a Spanish ally of Almagro, but the Spaniard stabbed him to death. Some friend.

TERRIFIC TEMPLES

When the conquistadors arrived in Cuzco they could scarcely believe their eyes. In fact conquistador Pedro de Cieza de Leon said …

> *If I wrote down everything I saw then no one would believe me!*

But in his book *Chronicle of Peru* he wrote down enough to give a glittering glimpse into the strange world where they came, they saw and they robbed.

> *We reached their Coricancha, the Incan House of the Sun. Around the wall, half-way up, was a band of gold, two palms wide and four fingers thick. The many doorways and the doors were covered in gold and inside the walls were four houses. The houses were not very large but each was covered with plates of gold on the outside and the inside.*

No wonder the greedy Spanish eyes popped out!

But the Incas didn't just cover their Sun Temple with gold. They were also great artists and filled the palace with golden models. Imagine Madame Tussaud's where everything is made of gold instead of wax!

In one of the temple houses was the figure of the sun, large and made of gold. It was cleverly made and studded with precious stones.

They also had a garden, but the soil was made from golden nuggets, and solid golden corn grew there. There were twenty llamas with their lambs, shepherds guarding them with slings and crooks – every single thing made of gold.

There were huge numbers of jars and pots and vases, all made of gold or silver and studded with emeralds.

And, in the Incan world every scrap of gold belonged to just one man: the Emperor. The Spanish planned to change that completely ... and for ever. They stripped off the gold, melted down the statues and shipped the lot back to Spain!

Savage sacrifices

What did the Incas actually *do* in their Sun Temple? They made sacrifices to their sun god. If you can build a gold-plated palace, 100 metres long and 30 metres wide, then you can try this for yourself ...

HOLY SMOKE

You too can be a perfect priest if you follow these simple instructions!

Sacrifice of the Day

First you need to make sure our Lord Sun appears each day, don't you? Then you'd better do the corn sacrifice each and every day ... or else it's goodnight to daylight!

First light a nice hot fire.

Then scatter corn on the fire and toast it.

As the corn toasts, chant,

EAT THIS, LORD SUN, SO YOU WILL KNOW WE ARE YOUR CHILDREN!

Then step outside and watch the sun come up.

No one knows why this works but it does ... every time!

Sacrifice of the Month

On the first day of each month, take a hundred pure white llamas.

Lead your llamas round to the images of the gods.

Divide the llamas among the thirty priests of the temple (one priest for each day of the month).

Massacre the llamas, throw chunks of their flesh on to the fire, then grind their bones into powder for use in your services.

Yes, those cute little bundles of fur, guinea pigs, were turned into guinea pork as sacrifices. But don't cringe too much. There are worse things than roasting pets, as you're about to find out. But first ...

Did you know ...?
When an emperor died the Incas would often pluck out *his eyebrows* and throw them to the wind as a gift to the gods. Goodness knows what the gods would do with them! Maybe make eyebrow wigs of their own?

OH GREAT. MORE EYE-BROWS. JUST WHAT I NEEDED...

Killing kids

If the Incas were in desperate trouble – defeat in battle, famine or plague – only *human* blood was good enough to bribe the gods. And the purest blood was a child's blood. The Incas believed their gods preferred a nice sweet kid!

Cold graves

The Incas made their human sacrifices up in the mountains. Germs don't like the thin mountain air – they can't afford oxygen masks – and the constant cold is like a fridge. So the child sacrifices haven't rotted away. They are still there to be found after 500 years.

A newspaper report in April 1999 described one find, an Incan sacrifice in Argentina …

She was found 22,000 feet up on the summit of the Lullaillaco volcano in the north-west Argentine Andes. The 500-year-old girl's face looks peaceful in spite of the way she died. They got her drunk on beer and she was numb with the cold before she was wrapped in blankets and brightly coloured cloth. Then she was buried alive.

The little Incan girl's face is the best preserved of any ever found. She and another boy and girl were naturally mummified by the extreme cold and lack of oxygen.

Scans have shown that their organs are not damaged, there appears to be frozen blood in their veins and the remains of their last meals are still in their bowels. The girl, whose face can be seen poking through the dusty rags, was about 14. Her cheeks are swollen but she looks like one of the dark-skinned children who play in the streets of Salta today, in the shadow of the mountain their ancestors worshipped.

Happy gods mean sunny days

It sounds incredibly cruel to take a child to the top of a mountain then bury them alive. But the Incas believed they were doing the right thing. If you asked an Incan priest they would have given you reasons ...

So children went to a gruesome death to keep a god happy. Very often the sacrifices were made as a way of saying 'Thank you!' to a god for a great victory in battle.

Terror for teenies

The journey to the top of the mountain took days, with stops every night in bare stone shelters.

Did the children know that death was waiting for them at the top of that mountain? In spite of the beer they had to dope them, the children must have been terrified.

An archaeologist described one find …

> The crown of the boy's skull is as bare as an eggshell. His adult teeth are just coming through. There is a crack caused by a heavy blow that killed him. Through the crack you can see his shrunken brain. But he still has a face and it looks twisted with what looks like fear.

Was it fear? Or was that just the imagination of the archaeologist?

Grave robbers

The child sacrifices were buried with a small supply of food, so they'd have something to eat on the journey to the next world. They were also buried with sea shells and gold figures of men, women and llamas.

The Spanish conquered Tahuantinsuyu in order to steal Incan gold, and treasure-hunters *still* wreck old graves to steal the golden images. They don't care about the history they are destroying and they certainly don't have any respect for the poor dead children. An archaeologist came across one grave that had been blown apart with dynamite …

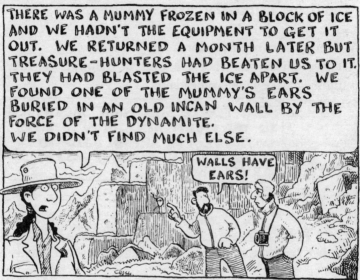

THERE WAS A MUMMY FROZEN IN A BLOCK OF ICE AND WE HADN'T THE EQUIPMENT TO GET IT OUT. WE RETURNED A MONTH LATER BUT TREASURE-HUNTERS HAD BEATEN US TO IT. THEY HAD BLASTED THE ICE APART. WE FOUND ONE OF THE MUMMY'S EARS BURIED IN AN OLD INCAN WALL BY THE FORCE OF THE DYNAMITE. WE DIDN'T FIND MUCH ELSE.

WALLS HAVE EARS!

The statues are often sold to rich collectors so they can't be seen in museums where the rest of us can study them. It isn't only the Incas and the conquistadors who are ruthless, greedy and selfish.

Pointy heads
Some of the child victims have been found with strange-shaped heads. It seems that they had wood strapped to their heads from the moment they were born so the infant heads were forced to grow to a point. The head took on the shape of the mountain on which they'd be sacrificed!

227

What if the mountain had twin peaks? Then the Incan parents managed to bind the children's heads in such a way that the skull grew into two peaks! Horrible but true!

And, after all that effort, they killed them.

Modern mummy murders

Archaeologists who visit the sites to examine sacrificed mummies make a gruesome claim …

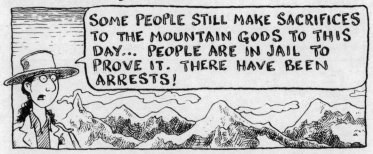

SOME PEOPLE STILL MAKE SACRIFICES TO THE MOUNTAIN GODS TO THIS DAY… PEOPLE ARE IN JAIL TO PROVE IT. THERE HAVE BEEN ARRESTS!

Another visitor to the Incan lands that are now in Argentina said …

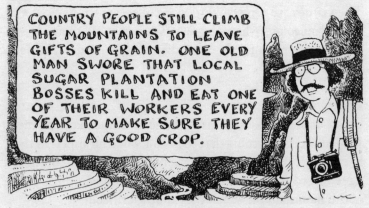

COUNTRY PEOPLE STILL CLIMB THE MOUNTAINS TO LEAVE GIFTS OF GRAIN. ONE OLD MAN SWORE THAT LOCAL SUGAR PLANTATION BOSSES KILL AND EAT ONE OF THEIR WORKERS EVERY YEAR TO MAKE SURE THEY HAVE A GOOD CROP.

Which is a bit like a head-teacher killing and eating a pupil every year to make sure they have good exam results! Let's hope no head–teacher reads this book.

Did you know …?
You may think the Incas were bloodthirsty, but some of the other tribes in Tahuantinsuyu were worse. The Spanish Friar Valverde, who baptized Atahuallpa, tried to flee when Francisco Pizarro was assassinated. He got to Ecuador, but was captured by Indians in Puná, who killed him … then ate him. (They probably sold him at a Friar Tuck shop.)

Llucky llama

In April each year the Incas had a ceremony in honour of Napa – the white llama. A white llama was dressed in a red shirt and had gold ear ornaments attached. He drank chicha beer and chewed coca leaves, the same as the priests.

Then he made a chicha sacrifice to the gods. How on earth can a llama make a sacrifice? Pots of chicha were laid out in the temple and the llama was sent in to kick them over! (Bet you wouldn't have thought of that!) And the biggest treat for the llama wasn't the beer … it was the fact that the priests let him live. The Napa llama was never sacrificed!

Other llamas weren't so lucky …

- two 'red' llamas were always sacrificed at a wedding
- 100 llamas were sacrificed every month at the Sun Temple
- thousands of llamas were sacrificed to the gods before a big battle

What if there were a drought or a famine? What would the people do?

That's an awful llot of llama.

And you really wouldn't want to know how the priests went about sacrificing a llama, would you? You would? Oh, very well, they slit their throats. (And that makes a right mess on a white llama's coat.)

And you really wouldn't want to know what the priests did with the blood, would you? You would? You *are* sick! If you must know the priest drank some of the blood and scattered the rest on the ground.

Did you know …?
Modern visitors to the ancient sacrifice site at Mount Sara Sara can stock up with food for the journey. In the villages at the foot of the mountain you can buy dried frogs. This is to make that popular dish, frog soup. If that's what you enjoy then hop over to Peru!

GROOVY GODS

Who were these gods who had to be kept supplied with fresh meat? The Incan gods could be grim and gruesome – like a lot of gods in a lot of countries. Here are a few for you to worship if you feel like it.

Viracocha
Job: Creator of Earth, humans and animals.
You may like to use one of his other names ...

- Lord Instructor of the World (Sounds like he was a head-teacher!)
- The Ancient One (Yes ... definitely a head-teacher!)
- The Old Man of the Sky.

Tall tales: Viracocha not only made humans – he also destroyed them, made them again out of stone, then scattered them around the world. After teaching humans how to survive he took his cloak, made it into a boat and sailed off into the Pacific Ocean.

Some Incas said that was a silly story ...

Viracocha was a good friend to the Incas. When Emperor Pachacuti was under attack by the Chanca, Viracocha appeared

231

to him in a dream and encouraged the Emperor on to victory. Pachacuti made a temple to Viracocha in Cuzco to say 'Thanks'. Appearance: Pachacuti had the god's image made in gold. This figure was about the size of a 10–year-old child. Was Viracocha a small god? Or was Pachacuti just a bit mean with the gold?

Inti
Job: Sun god.
He is named after an Incan emperor called Inti, which means 'My Father', because Inti was thought to be the parent of the Incan lords.
Appearance: A human face on a golden disc with sun-rays around the edge.

Mama-Kilya

Job: Moon mother and wife of Inti
Tall tales: The Incas believed that when Mama Moon cried her tears fell as silver. (A very handy mama to have if you need some extra pocket money! Chop an onion under her nose and get enough to buy a new computer game!)

Apu Illapu
Job: Rain-giver and god of thunder.
This was the god the common people prayed to mostly because rain was so important to them.
Terrible tales: Temples to Apu were usually in high places. When the people needed rain they climbed up to the temple and made a sacrifice. This was often a human sacrifice. It was a sort of straight swap – a human life for a shower of rain. (If

your grandad's cabbage patch needs some rain then you may like to sacrifice a history teacher to Apu and see if it works.)

Appearance: You can't see Apu but you can see his shadow – it's the band of stars we call the Milky Way. The Incas believed Apu took his water from the Milky Way. (That's daft, of course, because it would rain Milky Rain if it was true. The streets would be covered in butter!)

Pray-time

The Incas had priests and temples in every corner of their empire and a chief priest in Cuzco who was nearly as powerful as the Emperor.

As well as a temple you could pray at a 'huaca' – that's a holy place. But this holy place could be …

- a mountain
- a bridge
- a mummy (especially the mummy of a dead emperor)
- a cairn (a pile of stones by the side of a road – add a stone and the gods will grant you a safe journey).

Mummy magic

Going into battle? Then you need the help of the dead Incan emperors. Here's how to get it …

233

1 Take out their mummies and parade them in front of the warriors. (There was no mummy of the first emperor, Manco Capac, who turned to stone when he died.)

2 Get a military band to play music on bone flutes (made from human shin-bones) and tambourines.

3 Have poets recite long epic poems about the dead emperors. You may want to try this when your school next does battle with a rival school in soccer, hockey, netball or tiddlywinks. Parade your mummies while the school orchestra plays and recite an Incan epic. If you don't know any Incan epics then make one up, something like this ...

HERE'S OUR MUMMY, SINCHI ROCA,
TRY TO STOP US AND WE'LL CHOKE YER!
AND THE MUMMY OF OUR LLOQUE,
WE CAN'T LOSE WITH THIS GREAT BLOKE!
MAYTA IS THE NEXT IN LINE,
WE WILL BEAT YOU EVERY TIME.
FOLLOWED BY THE GREAT YUPANQUI,
WE WILL STOP YOUR HANKY PANKY!
INCA ROCA IS THE NEXT,
WHEN WE BEAT YOU, YOU'LL BE VEXED!
SEE THE FAMOUS LORD HUACAC,
HE'LL BE WITH US IN ATTACK!
VIRACOCHA, MIGHTY LORD,
HE'LL CHEER WHEN WE'VE SCORED!

Scary! No wonder the Incas won most of their battles!

234

Make that mummy

The emperor mummies were different to the sacrifice mummies that are found frozen on the mountain tops today. The emperor mummies were prepared more like Egyptian mummies. Their insides were taken out and they were stuffed with herbs. The eyes were then taken out (nice job for someone) and replaced with shells that were made to look like eyes.

The emperor's mummy was then stored carefully and well looked after by a team of servants. They made sure their mummy-monarch had …

- regular changes of clothes
- a cloth laid with his favourite food each day
- a special treat … visits from the most beautiful of the Chosen Women from the temple.

It was never boring being an emperor's mummy. As well as getting out and about in parades he would also be visited by the royal family who wanted advice. All in all it was a hectic and tiring life being dead.

Horrible horoscopes

The Incas believed that life was controlled by the gods and you had to check with them before you did anything. With the help of the priests you could …

- discover a criminal
- tell who would win a battle
- find the cure for a sickness.

The best place to chat to a god was at an 'oracle', a place where the god would make himself known. The oracle at the Huaca-chaca bridge must have looked a bit weird. A conquistador described it like this …

THE ORACLE WAS A WOODEN POLE AS THICK AS A FAT MAN. IT HAD A GOLDEN BELT AROUND THE WAIST AND TWO GOLDEN MOUNDS LIKE A WOMAN'S BREASTS!

A SORT OF TREASURE CHEST, THEN?

The Incas spoke to the oracle and the spirit of the river spoke back to them. (A pole as thick as a fat man could have held a

WHAT MUST I DO, OH GREAT ORACLE?

HOP IT, I'M STARVING!

priest as fat as a thin man inside, couldn't it? The priest could answer the question – then get to eat the sacrifice when the Incas had gone.) This may sound very artistic and charming. It wasn't. Spanish visitors reported that these 'oracles' were spattered with blood from sacrifices – often human blood.

Here are some other ways to find out about the future …

Faking firemen

It wasn't just priests at oracles who could cheat. There were men called *yacarca* who would speak to the spirits in a fire and answer your questions. They blew through a tube to make the fire glow red hot. The fire spirits then 'spoke' to anyone who wanted an answer to a question. But a clever-clogs conquistador spotted that the *yacarca* was actually a 'ventriloquist' – speaking the fire-spirit answers without moving his lips!

Coca crawlers

Another way to tell the future was to look at a dish of leaves picked from the coca plant. (A bit like reading the future by looking at tea leaves in a cup as some people still do today.) You could also take a powerful drugged drink called *ayahuasca* and see the future in the wild dreams it gave you. But strangest of all was to watch the way a spider wandered across the floor. That would tell you everything you wanted to know!

Llama lungs

Watching spiders not strange enough for you? Then try this ...

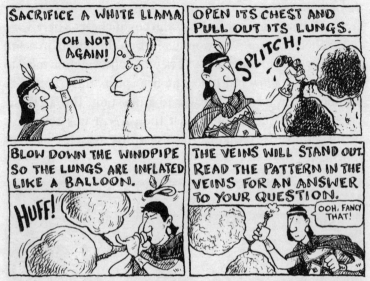

Remember, it must be a *white llama*. Next-door's cat is just not good enough.

Strange signs

An ancient Incan story said that one day strangers would land in Peru and destroy both the Incas and their religion. Emperor Huayna was worried, but especially when in 1532 he received more 'signs' from the gods ...

- At the Feast of the Sun an eagle appeared, chased by a flock of buzzards, and fell at the Emperor's feet. The priests fed and cared for it but the eagle died. What was the meaning? If the king of birds could be destroyed then so could an emperor?

- There were an unusual number of earthquakes. Great rocks shattered, mountains crumbled and tidal waves swamped the shores. What was the meaning? If a mountain could fall then so could an emperor?

- Comets filled the sky and the moon appeared to have three rings of light around it – one blood-red, one greenish-black and one smoky-grey. Of course the moon was believed to be the Emperor's mother. What was the meaning? A priest explained to the Emperor …

THE BLOOD-RED RING AROUND YOUR 'MOTHER' MEANS THAT WHEN YOU DIE A CRUEL WAR WILL BREAK OUT AMONGST YOUR PEOPLE. BLOOD WILL BE SHED IN STREAMS. THE BLACK RING MEANS THAT NOTHING WILL SURVIVE OF OUR RELIGION. EVERYTHING WILL VANISH IN SMOKE – THAT IS THE THIRD RING!

Three years later Huayna died, the Spanish had arrived with a new religion and the priest's words came true. Amazing! (Bet you wish that predicting-priest was around today. He could tell you next Saturday's lottery numbers!)

So how did the Incas think they might avoid their dreadful fate? By keeping the gods happy with lots of sacrifices: when Huayna died the Incas killed four *thousand* people to be buried with him. (And a fat lot of good it did them.) All because of a dead bird, a few earthquakes and a ring round the moon.

Fossil fuel

Who was the most important member of an Incan family? Dad? No. Mum? No. Mummy? Yes!

The ancient founder of a family – like your great-great … grandad – would have been turned into a mummy and was the family's most valuable member. In fact if another family kidnapped your mummy it could be held to ransom!

The Spanish arrived and were shocked at the way the Incas worshipped their ancestors. What did the conquistadors do with the mummies?

a) gave them a Christian burial

b) burned them

c) turned the mummies into shop–window dummies

Answer: **b)** Don't try this with your grandad … especially if he's not dead yet.

Good God

Once the Incan emperors had been defeated the Incas squabbled among themselves. Some rebelled and some made friends with the Spanish invaders. Inca killed Inca and Spaniard killed Spaniard as they fought over land and gold and religion.

The Spanish tried to make the Incas worship the Christian God, rather than Incan gods and mummies. But just when the plan seemed to be working a Spanish priest made a horrifying discovery. He told the governor the shocking news. His letter may have read something like this …

Parinacochas Village
Peru
21 June 1564

Your Grace,

The whole of Peru is in terrible danger. I discovered the truth here in my own parish. Send help at once. Send soldiers. Send arms.

I had noticed that the Indian men in my village disappeared every night to a large meeting hut. They wouldn't let me in! Me! Their priest! But I waited till they were all inside and listened at the door.

First they began to pray, and I realized they were praying to their old Incan gods. If that wasn't bad enough, one of their leaders (Curacas as they called them) stood up and began to scream at them. I remember his evil words now.

'The Christians have one God, they say. But we Incas have many more powerful ones. We also have hundreds and thousands of ancestors who care

PTO →

241

for us. They have told us that the Incan gods are going to rise up and destroy the Christian God! Floods will be sent to wash away all traces of the Spanish. We can start again. The Spanish will die. So will any Incas who follow them. If we Incas want to survive we must stop worshipping the Christian God and we must stop obeying the Spanish. Our gods are hungry and thirsty because Incas have stopped giving them Chicha beer and sacrifices. We must start again!'

The Incas say their gods are coming down from the hills and taking over their bodies. Some of these 'possessed' people shake, tremble and fall, or dance insanely.

After their meeting I took one of the weaker villagers and said I would burn him if he didn't tell me everything. It seems this rebel movement is spreading across Peru. We must destroy their holy places and burn their mummies. If we don't we will all die. In God's name, send help! Send help!

Your devoted servant,
Father Luis de Olivera

The Spanish sent investigators and discovered the rebellion was spreading fast. It took them three years to destroy all the holy places (huacas) they could find. They also destroyed 8,000 Incan rebels. The rebellion failed. Their mummies had let them down!

Purify that priest

The Incas found it painful to rebel against the Spanish Christians. Rebel Incas went on doing it in secret. These Incas thought Spanish priests made the Tahuantinsuyu ground impure by walking on it. So, after the priests had gone, they used a horribly historical way of cleaning their pathways ...

CLEANSE THAT CHRISTIAN

Has an unclean Christian walked your way today? Then purify your path the dead-dog way! Here's a handy hint from our happy huacas:

1. Catch a black dog. It must be black all over for this to work.

2. Tie its legs and drag it through the streets where the putrid priest has strutted.

3. Take the dog to the river and kill it.

4. Throw the dead dog into the water at a place where two rivers meet.

SPLOSH

5. It is now safe to walk your streets.

Don't try this at home! Dead dogs in rivers can pollute the water, kill the fish and make drinking water dreadful.

A 1613 revolt against the Catholic Church was crushed by the Spanish and the leaders arrested. These Incan leaders were so upset they poisoned themselves rather than become Christians.

And when one Incan leader (a Curaca) failed to support his people they poisoned him. But that sort of violence was rare. Most Incas pretended to be Christians but went on worshipping the Incan gods too.

Terrible tales

Do you have a really grotty little brother or sister? Offer to read them a little good-night story … then tell them this terrifying tale from Peru. The Spanish brought their superstitions as well as their religion to Peru, including a dreadful fear of cats who were thought to be mixed up in witchcraft and black magic.

Are you comfortable, dear little brother (or sister)? Then I'll begin.

Once upon a time in Peru there was a six-year-old boy called Jose. Now, Jose had a cruel and wicked grandfather called Manuel. The grandfather drank lots of strong wine at the local tavern but that didn't make him happy! No, it put him into a terrible temper and he could be really nasty. (He also had very smelly feet, but that's not important so I won't mention it.)

One night Grandfather Manuel staggered back from the local tavern in a terrible rage.

'I'm in a terrible rage!' he roared.

'W-w-w-why?' Jose asked.

Grandfather Manuel frowned and his ugly face twisted in disgust. It was as if someone had stuck his smelly feet under his nose. 'Don't ask stupid questions!' he roared. 'Ooooh! Me chest!' he gasped.

The old man's eyes popped, his knees flopped, his tongue swelled, his feet smelled and he fell forward, flat on his ugly face, dead!

'Ooooh! What a shame!' the people of the village wailed on the streets.

'Yippee!' the people of the village cheered when they were alone in their homes.

That was until they heard about the strange will he had written before he died. Grandmother Consuela read it to little Jose (who was a bit too young to read).

I, Manuel, order that the following must be done when I die:

1. My funeral to be held at midnight.
2. My coffin to be left open.
3. There must be enough chairs for all the people who will want to come.
4. My body must not be taken to church and there must be no priest at the funeral.

Grandmother Consuela quivered and Jose shivered. 'I can smell the fires of Hell in this!' the old woman wailed.

'I thought it was the smell of his feet,' her grandson sighed.

The evil smell filled the room where the coffin lay. No one came to visit the corpse – who can blame them?

At midnight a distant church bell rang. In the trembling silence a black cat stalked into the room. It had eyes as red as the coals of Hell. It was followed by a second cat, then a third and more. Soon every chair in the room was filled by a black cat with red eyes.

Grandmother Consuela whispered, 'Black cats are sent by the devil himself!'

'Why?' Jose asked.

'To claim the soul of the dead!' she croaked.

'His sole? The soles of his feet? Is that why they smell so bad?' the boy asked.

Before she could reply a cat started to wail and soon every cat in the room joined in to make a fearful noise like a school violin lesson.

The candles flickered and there was a soft creaking of the coffin. Grandfather Manuel sat up. His eyes were lifeless as ever but his body moved. First one smelly foot, then the other, was swung over the side of the coffin and the corpse stood on stiff legs.

The black cats marched from the room, tails held high, and the corpse shuffled out behind them.

'Where's Grandfather Manuel going?' little Jose asked.

Grandmother Consuela chewed her knuckles and mumbled. (You'd mumble too if you had a mouthful of knuckle.) 'He was an evil man in life, now his punishment is to have no peace in death. The devil has made Grandfather a *condenando* … he must wander the earth for ever more, never sleep and never rest!'

'Ooooh! That's horrible,' Jose sighed.

Grandmother Consuela jabbed a bony finger at the boy. 'And that's what'll happen to you if you are wicked or cruel to your big brother (or sister)! The black cats will come to get you!'

When you've finished the story your really grotty little brother or sister will have learned an important lesson from Spanish Peru. If they ever dare to upset you again all you have to say (as they say to nasty nippers in Peru to this day) is, 'Is that a black cat I see over there?'

INCA MYSTERY QUIZ

An Inca would look at you and think, 'Goodness me! These 21st century people are strange! They kill one another with metal machines called "cars"! Children play games with moving pictures where they learn to massacre hundreds of people on machines called "computers"! They have delicious meat but mash it up and fry it till it tastes like a dung-beetle's birthday cake and they call it a "burger"!'

There's nothing odd about Incan life – it's just that it looks that way to you. So here is a perfectly sensible Inca quiz …

1 The Incan people liked to keep their dead kings happy. How?
a) They fed them lots of beer so they could be Incan drinkas.
b) They put the latest books in the grave so they could be Incan thinkas.
c) They changed the shoes on the kingly corpses every week because they didn't want them to be Incan stinkas.

2 We call everyone who lived in the Empire 'Incas' today. But in those days 'Inca' was a word that was used for what?
a) Only the men (because women didn't matter)?
b) Only the people of Cuzco (because conquered people didn't matter).
c) Only the royal family (because no one else mattered).

3 The Incan Empire of Pachacuti stretched from the Amazon rainforest in the east almost to the Pacific Coast in the west. Why did the Incas not settle on the west coast?

a) Because it was too wet.

b) Because it was too dry.

c) Because they were afraid that sea monsters would jump out and eat them.

4 An Incan emperor wore a 'poncho' coat just once. What happened to each of these ponchos once he'd finished with it for the day?

a) They were given to the poor to keep them warm.

b) They were sacrificed to the gods.

c) They were stored in a special poncho palace.

5 Cuzco, like much of the Incan homelands, was 4,000 metres above sea level where the air is thin and most humans would struggle to breathe. How did the Incas manage?

a) They had really big strong hearts for pumping what little oxygen there was around their bodies.

b) They had big noses and big mouths so they could gulp down more air than most people.

c) They had big air tanks like aqualungs (made from llama skin) that they filled each day with lowland air and carried home to breathe.

6 How did the Incan men get rid of their facial hair?

a) They smothered their whiskers in honey and put their face in an anthill. The ants chewed off the honey and the hair. (That's a sweet idea.)

b) They shaved using razors made from sharp sea shells. (Shore is a good idea.)

c) They pulled their whiskers out one at a time using bronze tweezers. (They needed to be pretty plucky!)

7 When an Inca killed an enemy what could he use the dead man's skin for?

a) To cover a drum … so the enemy will be beaten twice! (Boom! Boom!)

b) To wrap some sandwiches for the journey home.

c) To scrape thin enough to let light through and use as a window in the family home.

8 An Incan princess died accidentally on a hunting trip. Her heartbroken Incan love, Illi Yunqui, buried his dead princess in the Lake of the Incas, high in the Andes. It is said that the water changed colour as her corpse splashed in and it's still that colour today. What colour?

a) Red, from her blood.

b) Green, the colour of her eyes.

c) Gold, the colour of the jewellery buried with her.

9 What nickname did the Spanish conquistadors give to the Incas when they first met them?
a) Big Ears.
b) Noddies.
c) Mr Plods.

10 A conquistador rode up to Emperor Atahuallpa and stopped just short of trampling him – it was meant to show how powerful the Spanish were. Atahuallpa didn't so much as blink … but some of his warriors did. How did Atahuallpa reward the warriors who had shown so much fear for their Emperor?
a) He gave them each their weight in gold for being so loyal.
b) He gave them a painful death for being cowards.
c) He gave them a llama to practise trick-riding like the Spanish.

Answers:

1a) The Incan lords made some peasants produce extra grain to brew into beer. This beer was then 'fed' to the mummies of the dead kings who probably became dead drunk as a result.

2c) Only the royal family were 'Incas' in Incan times. The Lord of Cuzco himself had the title 'Sapa' Inca – meaning 'King'. There were never more than 1,800 pure-blood Incas of the royal family. But, when they ran short of a royal to rule they could 'adopt' a trusted outsider. These 'adopted' Incan royals were called 'Hahua' Incas.

3b) The shoreline of the Pacific was dry and not suitable for growing crops. It's said that anyone living there might see a shower of rain once or twice *in their lifetime*! The Incas probably could have conquered it if they'd really wanted.

4b) The poncho was taken to a temple where it was burned as a sacrifice to the gods. You may like to try this with your dad's smelly socks.

5a) Incan hearts could carry 60% more blood round the body than the average human. And blood carries oxygen to the brain and the muscles that need it. The air was thin but the Incan people got more of it. (And put on a dunce's cap and go to the bottom of the class if you answered **c**).) The Incas also seemed to survive the cold better. A Spanish monk, Barnabe Cobos said …

I'm amazed at how warm the Incas are in the coldest weather, and how they can sleep on snow a palm's width deep. They lie on it as if it was a feather bed. I believe the reason is they have stomachs as tough as an ostrich's!

Uh?

6c) Incan men plucked their facial hair out with bronze tweezers. These tweezers were so valuable to them they were buried with their owners. That's a good idea and it must work because you never see an Incan mummy with a beard!

7a) The Incas went into battle playing drums and tambourines made with the skin of dead enemies.

8b) The lake is green, said to be the colour of her eyes. (No one has trawled the lake for her corpse to find out if she really did have green eyes. Anyway the fish have probably scoffed them.) It is said that on still winter nights you can still hear the moans of her heartbroken love. (More likely to be some tourist moaning, 'My God, it's cold up here! I wish I'd worn me thermal knickers!')

9a) They called them Big Ears because of the way the Incas stretched their ear lobes to wear big ornaments.

10b) An example of how Atahuallpa's soldiers were treated very strictly. They always did what they were told. So, when Atahuallpa told them not to harm the conquistadors they didn't. They didn't fight back when the conquistadors began to massacre them! Atahuallpa's ruthless rule backfired on him.

EPILOGUE

No one says the Incan emperors were kind rulers. But the Incan people suffered far, far more under the Spanish conquistadors.

The Incan way of life had some good ideas. They said that everyone should help everyone else with everything. The government tried to make sure that this happened. Life would be so much easier if that happened today!

The Incas also had some pretty dodgy ideas. They believed in Heaven and Hell like their Spanish conquerors, but they were a little different. Heaven was the sun where the good people went for warmth and food – Hell was inside the Earth where the bad suffered cold and hunger. So children, who were too young to be evil, would go to Heaven and happiness ... and by burying a child sacrifice alive you were doing the child a favour!

But they lived in a harsh world where earthquakes and landslides could destroy all they'd spent years building, where it could take days to walk just a few miles and where survival depended on the warmth and the kindness of the sun. It was a brutal world so it's not surprising there could be brutal people in it.

Pachacuti was one of the greatest ever native Americans. As he lay dying he managed to be quite poetic about his fate ...

Like a lily in the garden I was born,
Like a lily I grew up.
Years passed, I grew old.
I withered and died.

He could have been writing about the tribes who inhabited the Andes before the Incas. He could have been writing about the Incan nation itself. He could have been writing about the conquistadors.

All a bunch of lilies.

A bitter Incan survivor of the conquest wrote a poem to his gods about the fate of the Incas ...

> *You are lying spirits,*
> *You are cruel and devilish enemies.*
> *You are the cause of my misery and my failure!*
> *I have adored you with all my power,*
> *I have worshipped you with great sacrifices,*
> *With human sacrifices.*
> *You are just greedy robbers*
> *And cruel enemies of my soldiers.*
> *You shall be cursed for what you have done.*
> *None of my children will worship you,*
> *Not even the tiniest girl-child,*
> *And not my royal grandchildren,*
> *I curse you for ever.*

All those men, women, children and llamas were sacrificed to the gods. In return they asked the gods to protect them and care for them.

The gods let them down.